Common-Sense
Classroom Management

**Techniques for Working With
Students With Significant Disabilities**

Jill A. Lindberg • Michele Flasch Ziegler • Lisa Barczyk

Foreword by Lou Brown

CORWIN PRESS
A SAGE Company

For information:

Corwin Press
A SAGE Company
2455 Teller Road
Thousand Oaks, California 91320
www.corwinpress.com

SAGE Ltd.
1 Oliver's Yard
55 City Road
London EC1Y 1SP
United Kingdom

SAGE India Pvt. Ltd.
B 1/I 1 Mohan Cooperative Industrial Area
Mathura Road, New Delhi
India 110 044

SAGE Asia-Pacific Pte. Ltd.
33 Pekin Street #02-01
Far East Square
Singapore 048763

Printed in the United States of America.

Library of Congress Cataloging-in-Publication Data

Lindberg, Jill A.
Common-sense classroom management techniques for working with students with significant disabilities/
Jill A. Lindberg, Michele Flasch Ziegler, Lisa Barczyk.
        p. cm.
Includes bibliographical references and index.
ISBN 978-1-4129-5818-9 (cloth)
ISBN 978-1-4129-5819-6 (pbk.)
    1. Classroom management. 2. Children with disabilities—Education. 3. Special education teachers—
In-service training. I. Ziegler, Michele Flasch. II. Barczyk, Lisa. III. Title.

LB3013.L553 2009
371.9—dc22   2008022890

This book is printed on acid-free paper.

08   09   10   11   12   10   9   8   7   6   5   4   3   2   1

Acquisitions Editor:	Jessica Allan
Editorial Assistant:	Joanna Coelho
Production Editor:	Libby Larson
Copy Editor:	Teresa Herlinger
Typesetter:	C&M Digitals (P) Ltd.
Proofreader:	Theresa Kay
Indexer:	Will Ragsdale
Cover Designer:	Michael Dubowe
Graphic Designer:	Michael Dubowe

■ Contents

■ Foreword

Assume we contacted all knowledgeable, experienced, reasonable, concerned, and relevant persons from all geographic areas, and ethnic, racial, and socio-economic levels. Then we asked them to delineate the skills, techniques, attitudes, values, and other important elements that should be in the repertoire of a good teacher of students with severe disabilities. Certainly, some of that which was delineated would be on lists associated with all teachers. Just as certainly, some of this information would be unique to those who teach the students of primary concern here.

After examining the list, most would realize that it is impossible for any one person to actualize all of the elements in an instructional program for even one student. But with this fund of knowledge available and with its appropriate implementation, the results would be a substantial enhancement of the basic life quality of students with disabilities. This book contains a compilation of important basic information related to the repertoire needed by those involved in the education of these students.

Who should be aware of this information? Who should help bring to life the imbedded goals, concepts, and strategies? Who can benefit from the contents?

Both new and experienced teachers who interact with students with significant disabilities should be aware of the contents. Why? Because they can use it as a guideline to help verify that they are implementing a credible array of important policies, values, and instructional practices.

Parents of children with significant disabilities should absorb the contents. Why? Because the book is written in a style that easily communicates basic information to individuals without a degree or any training in special education. Because parents who have this knowledge will be better advocates for their children within their schools and communities. Because they will have a standard by which to measure the services being provided for their child.

Higher education teacher training personnel should be familiar with this book. Why? Because it will provide them with an excellent resource for their neophyte teachers.

Finally, those who are involved in the various types of alternative teacher training programs should be aware of this book. Why? Because it will remind them that the teachers with whom they are involved must be held to the same high standards as teachers in a traditional teacher certification program.

This book, then, offers a readable and practical introduction to the basics of teaching children with significant disabilities—our most challenging and deserving students.

Lou Brown
Professor Emeritus
University of Wisconsin

■ Preface

Dear special education teacher,

Welcome to *Common-Sense Classroom Management Techniques for Working With Students With Significant Disabilities.* The focus of our book is to provide support, resources, and teaching strategies for educating students with unique learning characteristics. You will find practical ideas, Web-based resources, and easy-to-use documents to assist you in developing high-quality educational practices that will help your students achieve their full potential. The book is structured so that each chapter provides topic-centered information with implementation strategies that include specific examples. Most chapters include figures such as charts, graphs, resources, or sample forms that can be used as is or modified.

It is our belief that students with complex intellectual disabilities learn best when instruction follows a routine pattern and is provided in naturally occurring, age-appropriate settings. All students have a place in general education; special education is designed and intended to support the student in environments that are appropriate for the concept or skill being taught. Throughout this book, you will find examples of how to establish learning opportunities that are inclusive of students with and without disabilities.

Special education teachers have many responsibilities, and the laws driving our paperwork seem to change frequently. The aim of this book is to help you focus on the unique strengths and needs of the students you serve. You'll find practical ideas for organizing your work, tracking student progress, and coordinating the team of professionals working with each student. Any of the ideas you find here can be changed and modified to meet the unique needs of your school or community setting. We hope you find the strategies helpful to you and your students.

Best wishes for success this school year.

Jill Lindberg
Michele Ziegler
Lisa Barczyk

■ About the Authors

Jill A. Lindberg has a degree in Exceptional Education from the University of Wisconsin–Milwaukee. She retired from Milwaukee Public Schools in June 2003 and is currently a supervising teacher for the University of Wisconsin–Milwaukee. Her teaching experience includes 6 years as a mentor teacher assisting both general and special education teachers in Milwaukee Public Schools. She has also taught students with specific learning disabilities, students with emotional/behavioral disabilities, and students with hearing impairment.

This book is the fifth in the *Common Sense* series that she has coauthored with educators from the Milwaukee area.

Michele Flasch Ziegler has a PhD in Special Education from the University of Wisconsin–Madison as well as a Master's Degree in Education Administration from Indiana University. She has 19 years of experience in teaching, administration, and teacher training. Her teaching experiences include working as a high school classroom teacher for students with intellectual disabilities and as a transition teacher for the Madison, Wisconsin, Metropolitan School District. She also assisted in coordinating services and offering technical support to teachers working in the K–12 intellectual disabilities program in the Indianapolis Public Schools. Currently, she is an assistant professor at Cardinal Stritch University in Milwaukee, Wisconsin. In an effort to continually expand opportunities and the quality of life for individuals with intellectual disabilities, she continues to support schools and families that include individuals with diverse needs.

Lisa Barczyk is a physical therapist with 22 years of professional experience in school-based pediatric practice. After graduating from Marquette University, she took a position with Milwaukee Public Schools as a staff physical therapist, and for the past 12 years has served as the supervisor of occupational and physical therapy. In that role, she has developed and provided specialized training and support to teachers, therapists, and teaching assistants of students with significant and multiple challenges.

■ Introduction and Overview

Disability is a natural part of the human experience and in no way diminishes the right of individuals to participate in or contribute to society. Improving educational results for children with disabilities is an essential element of our national policy of ensuring equality of opportunity, full participation, independent living, and economic self-sufficiency for individuals with disabilities.

Individuals with Disabilities
Education Improvement Act of 2004 (IDEIA)

People with disabilities are a part of our society. We are not surprised to see individuals using walkers or wheelchairs in shopping centers, churches, entertainment venues, and schools. In some communities, crosswalks are designed with blinking lights and sound indicators for the safe crossing of those with hearing or vision loss. We find persons with cognitive disabilities working—sometimes with assistance—in our grocery stores or fast food restaurants; our colleges and universities are improving access and accommodation for students with disabilities. In our elementary and secondary schools, we find a wide variety of disabling conditions among the student body—some that will require special education services.

Defining Significant and Multiple Disabilities

Multiple disabilities means concomitant impairments (such as mental retardation-blindness or mental retardation-orthopedic impairment), the combination of which causes such severe educational needs that they cannot be accommodated in special education programs solely for one of the impairments. Multiple disabilities does not include deaf-blindness.

IDEIA 2004 (sec. 300.8)

Individuals with Disabilities Education Improvement Act of 2004 (IDEIA)

Students with multiple and significant disabilities comprise approximately 2% of all students enrolled in special education programs (National Center for Education Statistics, 2006). The occurrence of significant and multiple disabilities, while less frequent than other disabilities, will most likely be apparent in some residents of our communities. In our schools and as teachers, we must be especially vigilant about ensuring opportunity and participation for children with significant and multiple disabilities. Significant disability occurs when there are functional limitations in the following seven major life activities: self-care, receptive and expressive language, learning, mobility, self-direction, independent living, and economic self-sufficiency. Each of these areas will be explored more fully in subsequent chapters. In this book, teachers of students with multiple and significant disabilities will find practical, common-sense ideas and strategies that will help ensure the best possible educational outcomes for their students.

Disability From Birth Versus Acquired Disability

▶ A disability occurring from the time of birth is commonly referred to as a *developmental* disability. A disability that occurs later in life as a result of accident, injury, or a disease process is commonly referred to as an *acquired* disability. Most students with significant disabilities have a developmental disability; this means that their development has been delayed since birth and their abilities have not followed the typical sequence of skill acquisition.

▶ Some students with significant disabilities have an acquired disability. This means that they have had a period of early development that followed the typical sequence of skill acquisition. The age at which a child sustains an injury or disease process is directly related to the degree of disability that will result. For example, the most prevalent acquired disability resulting in significant and multiple disabilities in children or adolescents is traumatic brain injury (TBI). Severe brain injuries result from trauma in motor vehicle accidents, falls, or from external force such as in cases of abuse. Children sustaining a severe brain injury younger than age 7 are less likely than older children to recover cognitive abilities (Anderson, Catroppa, Morse, Haritou, & Rosenfeld, 2005).

▶ Does it matter if the disability is developmental or acquired? Expectations matter. Following an acquired disability, families and educators may anticipate the return of skills the child previously had mastered. This is a valid approach to rehabilitation for a period of up to 24 months.

▶ Similarly, families and educators of a child with a developmental disability may expect the child to follow the developmental sequence no matter how long it takes to achieve motor and learning milestones. This is a valid approach to habilitation until it becomes clear, generally before age 5, that the child's skills are not following the typical sequence of development.

▶ When significant disability is present beyond age 5 or for 2 years following an injury or disease, the focus of educational interventions must change so that the child's most functional potential for life skills can be achieved.

Common Learning Characteristics

▶ Students with significant disabilities have learning styles, preferences, and personalities unique to themselves as individual learners. Some common characteristics observed in many students with significant disabilities can include the following:

a. Use of alternative communication methods due to absent or limited vocalized speech
b. Need for assistance with physical mobility
c. Difficulty with generalizing learned skills across environments
d. Need for repeated practice in order to learn and maintain skills
e. Learning less material at a slower rate
f. Reliance on tactile and multisensory learning experiences due to limitations in vision or hearing
g. Need for instruction and support for recreation, leisure, and vocational activities
h. Need for instruction and assistance for community access or community-referenced learning
i. Need for a blending of functional and academic curricula

Each of these learning characteristics will be explored more fully in the chapters that follow.

Dignity and Respect

▶ As educators of students with significant disabilities, we set an example for others by the ways in which we interact with our students. Our language, physical support, movement, and personal care of students must reflect the same degree of dignity and respect that would be offered to students without disabilities who are of the same age.

a. Language: Our students are people first, and our language must reflect that. Some examples of "person-first" language are listed in the following table.

Inappropriate Descriptors	Language With Dignity
The disabled	Persons (or people) with disability
Confined to a wheelchair	Uses a wheelchair
Normal child	Child without disability
Dumb, mute	Person who cannot speak; person who is non-verbal
Epileptic	Person with a seizure disorder
Retarded, slow, Down's kid	Child with a cognitive disability, child with Down syndrome, child with developmental delays
CP kid	Child with cerebral palsy
She's severe; he's profound	S/he has significant and multiple disabilities

b. Physical support: Students with significant disabilities often require external supports to maintain seated or standing positions in the classroom. At very young ages, it is appropriate to find children sitting on a teacher's lap. In elementary school as the child gets older, this practice becomes less appropriate. If second graders without disabilities do not sit on adults' laps, then second graders with disabilities should not do so. There are many types of adaptive equipment, such as standing frames, sidelyers, floor sitters, and bean bag chairs, that students can use while actively engaged in learning activities in the classroom.

c. Mobility: Most students with significant disabilities will use wheelchairs for mobility or will be dependent on others to facilitate movement throughout the school and community. It is important to prepare students for movement. Approach students from the side or the front to ask if they want to move, or when necessary, tell them they must move. For example, "Aneisha, it is time for lunch; we are going to move to the lunchroom." After a brief pause, begin moving the student's wheelchair. Do not say, "I have to move your chair," unless the student is not using his or her wheelchair at the time. Also, if you are going to provide physical assistance or prompting, always use a verbal cue to tell students you will be providing hand-over-hand assistance. When possible, this assistance should be provided from behind the student to support natural movement.

d. Health and safety: Our world has many dangers and risks; all students will be faced with situations in which they may not know which course of action to take. These situations are no different for people with significant disabilities. To ensure safety and good health for all students, even those with significant disabilities, health and safety issues need to be a priority in our teaching and must not be ignored. Students with significant disabilities need to learn how to use public transportation; how to acquire home and work safety skills such as reporting a fire, calling 9-1-1, and so forth; and how to acquire crime prevention skills. (See Chapter 4, Academic Planning, for further information.)

e. Self-determination: Like those without disabilities, people with significant disabilities have interests and preferences; however, they do not always have the opportunity to make choices and decisions based upon those preferences (Ryndak & Alper, 2003). Students with significant disabilities can participate in some parts of the decision-making and choice-making process. The ability to make a choice is a fundamental right for all persons and is the basis for learning and for developing relationships. Providing choices and following through on selections are methods of teaching that will maximize the student's participation in problem-solving activities and promote self-determination. (See Chapter 5, Functional Planning, under Self Advocacy and Self-Determination.)

f. Socialization and peer relationships: When asked to think about the important things in life, most people would place family relationships and friendships with others at the top of the list. Humans are social beings. Students with significant disabilities need to be provided the opportunity to develop relationships with peers both with and without disabilities. These social relationships can be facilitated in the general education environment and in community settings. (See Chapter 5, Functional Planning, under Social Skills and Peer Relationships.)

g. Personal care and hygiene: Students with significant disabilities will likely need assistance for daily routines such as dressing, eating, and using the bathroom. This will require an adult to be with the student at somewhat sensitive times during the school day. Keep in mind that adults perform these activities *with* the student, not *for* the student. Maintaining the dignity of the person is essential during these times of care:

Dressing	Eating and Meal Preparation	Toileting	Hygiene
Assist parents in selecting clothing that is loose fitting and age appropriate. Ensure that clothing is properly aligned for a neat appearance. Ensure that clothing is clean. Communicate with the student: comment on clothes, weather, transportation.	In lieu of bibs, use cloth napkins, paper towels, bandanas, large T-shirt, and so forth. Encourage decision making whenever possible (cup or spoon, fruit or meat, and so on). Use hand-over-hand assistance whenever necessary. Communicate with the student: comment on food items, previous meals, plans for the day.	Toileting tasks or menstrual care should be done in a private area in the bathroom. Keep personal items in cabinets or colored bins. Refer to diapers as "underwear." Communicate with the student: comment on the process—ready to lift, almost done, moving back to the wheelchair.	Grooming (bathing, washing face, brushing teeth, using deodorant, nail care, taking medication) should be done in a naturally occurring setting or private area. Keep personal items in cabinets or colored bins. When transporting these items in the hallway, use a backpack or canvas bag to ensure privacy. Provide consistent instruction at school and at home. Communicate with the student to encourage independence and evaluation of one's appearance.

1

Getting Ready

As a teacher of students with multiple and significant disabilities, you will need to be prepared and organized for the school year. There are several things to do before students arrive that will help you feel ready. Foremost, it is important to understand the diverse abilities and needs of your students. Armed with this information, you can then locate materials and resources that will be useful for them. Furthermore, it will be critical to develop relationships within your school and surrounding community. Why not start now?

Chapter Outline

- Time Organization

- Student Information

- Finding Appropriate Materials and Adaptive Equipment

- Physical and Visual Arrangements Within the Room

- Helping Administrators, General Education Teachers, and Support Staff Understand the Needs and Abilities of Students

- Knowing Your Community

Time Organization

The list of things that need to be done during the school year is a long one. It includes individualized education programs (IEPs), meeting with and training

support staff, ongoing communication with parents, and planning instruction. Meanwhile, you have the important job of teaching and supporting your students. You might begin to wonder how you're going to accomplish all of this. Here are some strategies to consider that will help you more efficiently organize your time and complete your many tasks.

▶ As a special education teacher, you have a good deal of paperwork and responsibility that goes beyond preparation for teaching. So, finding a system to organize forms and paperwork is very important. Make this a system that works for you. The use of baskets, totes, or other compact containers is one good way to do this. Another way is developing a file or binder system. Consider using your desk or designating a shelf near your desk for these important containers or binders. If you put them on your desk, think about using stackable containers to avoid clutter and to ensure work space. Listed below are some ways to organize the information and to divide pertinent paperwork, forms, and materials so they are at your fingertips.

   a. Things to complete today or for the week—This could include lesson plan materials, administrative or office requests, and so forth.
   b. Calls to make or people to contact—This might include parents, teachers, support staff, administrators, or community contacts.
   c. Academic activities and planning—This might include schedules, unit or lesson plans, ecological inventories, student profiles, IEPs-at-a-glance, copies of data sheets, and so forth. (See student information below.)
   d. Student behavior or medical needs and procedures to follow—This might include behavior intervention plans and medical response plans for seizures, gastrostomy tubes (G-tubes), asthma, and so forth.
   e. Important phone numbers—This could include agencies, administrators, support staff, therapist, individual student and family contact information, and so on.

▶ To save time in your busy day, make forms and templates that can be reproduced for continued use. Use lists with items that can be checked off or circled to save time rather than repeatedly writing tedious notes. Create forms for lessons, behavior, data collection for IEP objectives, and meetings. Using different-colored paper for the various forms or academic areas will make it easier for you to quickly access what you need. (See Figures 1.1, 1.2, and lesson plan data collection forms found in Chapter 2, Figures 2.7 and 2.8.) In addition, commercially made materials are available from a variety of vendors. See Figure 1.5 for a list of some of these.

▶ Also, develop a form to be completed by the general educators who teach your students that provides information and feedback on student progress or concerns for each week (see Figure 1.1). It is important to collaborate with general education staff to determine if the system that is developed is effective and not too time consuming. E-mail may be used to do this as well. Usually, special education teachers and support staff will remain with students with significant disabilities in the general education class. So face-to-face contact with staff can and should be used on a regular basis.

▶ Prioritize what needs to get done on a weekly basis. First, consider the ongoing communication and record keeping involved with individual student IEPs and the needs that should be documented and monitored. As you develop your master schedule, time should be blocked out for these weekly tasks to be completed. (See Chapter 2, Figures 2.4 and 2.5, for ideas on how to do this.) Also, consider if there is a specific time when things can or must be done. For example, face-to-face communication with general education teachers might need to occur before or after school. Developing a checklist for these tasks is also helpful. Keep it handy on your desk where you'll be sure to see it, or post it on a bulletin board near your desk. It's always a good feeling to check off a task that has been completed.

▶ Decide on a consistent time to meet and touch base with your instructional support staff on a weekly basis. This time should be used to review student progress, and to discuss instructional strategies and materials and decide if any changes need to be made. It's important for instructional staff to share ideas and be valued as members of the team.

▶ Continue to look for ideas for materials and instructional strategies. Create resource files or plastic labeled containers for materials and instructional ideas so that you have them at your fingertips. It may be necessary to create your own student-specific materials, and establishing space for a workstation may be helpful for organizing materials. See Figure 1.3 for examples of what to include in such a center.

Student Information

Every student with multiple and significant disabilities has unique abilities. As teachers, it is our responsibility to facilitate the student's use of these abilities in academic and functional settings. Students should also develop new skills so they can live, work, and play in an integrated community as independently as possible. Our number one job is to be aware of our students' strengths and needs in order to facilitate learning. The following tasks will give you a head start.

▶ Contact people who are relevant to the student's life. This should include but is not limited to past teachers, parents or guardians, siblings, and therapists. Give these people time to share information about the student and his or her strengths and needs. Information you might want to elicit from them could include the student's likes and dislikes, special equipment needed or used, medical needs, specific teaching strategies that have been successful with learning and managing behaviors, and things that are rewarding and motivating for the student. A *family inventory* is a tool or process that helps to identify skills the student with multiple and significant disabilities will need to obtain in order to more fully participate with the family, neighbors, and friends in daily or weekly activities at home or in the community. A variety of approaches can be used to gather information from families including the following: Personal Futures Planning (O'Brien, 1987), Making Action Plans (MAPS, Menchetti & Sweeney, 1995), and the MAPS Process (Falvey, Forest, Pearpoint, & Rosenberg, 1997). Some educators develop a survey-type tool for the family to complete. Several domains are discussed in the family inventory. Some of these include personal profile, home life, community activities, work or chores, general education curriculum

Figure 1.1 Quick Feedback Form

Student _____	**Week of** _____
Class _____	

> Please use this check-off or jot-down form to indicate how best I can assist the above student in your class. Please list any comments or concerns regarding student's progress.

1. Goals
   - Curriculum/Content
   - IEP

Meeting Expectations. . . . . . . Not Meeting				
(Progress)			(No Progress)	
1	2	3	4	5
1	2	3	4	5

2. Participation in Class

Active/Responsive . . . . Passive				
1	2	3	4	5

3. Behavior

Manageable . . . . Unmanageable				
1	2	3	4	5

4. Demands on Your Time

Reasonable . . . . Too Demanding				
1	2	3	4	5

5. Peer Connection

Connected . . . . Isolated				
1	2	3	4	5

6. Supports/Adaptations

Effective . . . . Not Effective				
			(Reevaluate)	
1	2	3	4	5

Comments:

If a support person is involved, should we consider fading out this support person or using him or her in a different way to support the class and all students?

❏ NO

❏ YES — If yes, how? _____

SOURCE: Adapted from *Wisconsin School Inclusion Project: Team Planning Packet* (1995).

Figure 1.2 IEP-at-a-Glance

	←List Class/Activity From Schedule →							
Student _____ Date/Semester _____ ↓ **Priority Goals/Objectives**								

SOURCE: Adapted from *Wisconsin School Inclusion Project: Team Planning Packet* (1995).

Figure 1.3 Teacher Workstation for Creating Classroom Materials

Item	Strategies	Resources
Computer: Desktop or laptop with CD burner, CD/DVD player, and speakers	Create and store classroom materials and resources Access Web-based materials: News-2-You Reading A–Z The Wiz (free)	School or School District www.news-2-you.com www.readinga-z.com www.ablenetinc.com
Computer Software: BoardMaker Writing with Symbols PowerPoint	Picture Schedule Communication Adapt text Create electronic books	Mayer-Johnson www.mayer-johnson.com
Color Printer	Quickly print, and use pictures, lessons, books	School or district/office supply stores
Digital Camera	Picture schedules Communication aids Personalized books Labels for classroom materials Lesson review Student positioning	Home or office supply stores
CD Player **iPod and speakers**	Record or play music and audio books Individual or group use	Office supply stores www.apple.com
Foam Core	Schedules Templates Games	Office supply stores Craft or hobby stores
Velcro Sticky-back strips Sticky-back dots or coins	Schedules Communication aids Games	Mayer-Johnson www.mayer-johnson.com Sammons-Preston www.sammonspreston.com
Cardstock (multicolor)	Mounting for pictures/symbols/schedules	School office

SOURCE: Lisa Barczyk, 2007.

in an inclusive classroom, general education learning priorities, future hopes and dreams, functional needs and priorities, peer relationships, community assessment, and related service needs.

▶ The students' IEPs are the most important documents you will draft and refer to throughout the year. Keep them in a safe place, and check the school policies regarding individual students' records. The actual IEP document might need to be stored in a secure location. You should have all necessary IEPs on the first day of school. If you don't, inform the principal or special education administrator in your building immediately. Specific information requiring close attention will include the following:

    a. Family members' or guardians' names and contact information (home and work phone numbers, emergency contact)
    b. Students' birth date, student ID number, IEP due date
    c. Particular behavior(s) and intervention strategies
    d. Medical needs, medication, or seizure disorder information, if applicable
    e. Physical disability or needs
    f. Transportation and other supplementary services or aides

The Individuals with Disabilities Education Improvement Act of 2004 (IDEIA) requires that students with significant disabilities have annual goals and short-term objectives written in the IEP. Furthermore, IDEIA specifies that, for students with disabilities who take alternate assessments aligned to alternate achievement standards (in addition to the annual goals), a description of benchmarks or short-term objectives is required.

▶ Review the IEP and each student's annual goals and objectives. Develop an IEP-at-a-glance such as the one in Figure 1.2 that can be kept on your desk in a binder or someplace you devise to organize forms and other information. The amount of time students should be included in general education, any special equipment needs, medical or feeding needs, behavior, and specific community experiences in which students should be involved should all be included in the IEP-at-a-glance. When appropriate, the IEP-at-a-glance can also be shared with general education teachers, therapist, and support staff who work with the student. Develop student profiles based on information from the IEP that include what you know and what you have learned about the student and his or her learning style. It's important to write profiles so as to discuss students' strengths and needs. As you develop these profiles, you should keep two questions in mind: What can the student do? What is the student working on? Profiles should be easily accessible and should be shared with general education teachers and other support staff. (See Figure 1.4 for a sample student profile.)

▶ As you look at IEPs, develop a domain list—a categorized list of instructional areas based on IEPs, including general education, domestic, community, vocational, recreation and leisure, and health and hygiene—labeled with the students' names and the objectives that fall under each domain. This list will help you when you create your master schedule. (See Chapter 2, Figures 2.4 and 2.5, for ideas.)

Finding Appropriate Materials and Adaptive Equipment

Finding appropriate materials, equipment, and supplies can be the biggest challenge for you as a teacher—especially as students get older. You will need age-appropriate materials that are understandable and not too abstract for students with significant disabilities. Start exploring resources and making materials, knowing that this will be an ongoing process. IDEIA defines equipment as

(a) Machinery, utilities, and built-in equipment, and any necessary enclosures or structures to house the machinery, utilities, or equipment; and (b) All other items

Figure 1.4   Student Profile

Student: Age: D.O.B. Grade: Teacher: Parent/Guardian: Phone: Siblings/Others at home:	<u>Documented Disability</u> <u>Health/Medical Information</u>

LIKES	DISLIKES	I learn best when . . .

I also want you to know that . . .	

Reading	**Writing** ☐ **Left-handed** ☐ **Right-handed**	Math

Work Habits and Self-Management		
Work Independently	**Organization and Managing Belongings**	**Assistance Needed With Eating, Hygiene, or Self-Care**

Communication

Social/Behavioral

Motor/Mobility

Other Information

SOURCE: Adapted from *Wisconsin School Inclusion Project: Team Planning Packet* (1995).

necessary for the functioning of a particular facility as a facility for the provision of educational services, including items such as instructional equipment and necessary furniture; printed, published, and audio-visual instructional materials; telecommunications, sensory, and other technological aids and devices; and books, periodicals, documents, and other related materials. (Sec. 300.14)

▶ Some students with significant disabilities may have specialized equipment for communication, educational, or therapy purposes. This equipment should be listed in the IEP, and the school district is required to provide access. Locate and become familiar with using this equipment before the students arrive. If there is something you can't find, contact your school administrator or special education administrator. It is imperative that appropriate equipment be available for the students on the first day of school.

▶ When students are included in general education classes, you need to become familiar with the curriculum, textbooks, workbooks, and other materials. Obtain a copy of the textbook(s) for each class, and try to get copies of the materials that will be used. To acquire a copy of these books, start by asking the general education teacher; then check with your building and district administrator. If you are lucky enough to obtain copies of the books and workbooks, guard them with your life so you will have them for future use. Be sure to familiarize yourself with what is taught and how the information is connected to state standards, benchmarks, or learning targets for that grade level. Also, be sure to look at the teacher's manuals, as many of them offer suggestion for reteaching or even modifying work. Locate materials and supplies that are age appropriate and as unobtrusive as possible. Teachers may need to adapt materials, especially written text, to include pictures and word symbols. This will be an ongoing process. (See Figure 1.5 for places to buy commercially made items.)

▶ Always use items such as photographs or line drawings to eliminate abstractness for student. For example, when teaching money, use real money instead of fake coins; take pictures in the school and community for a lesson on mapping; use real objects such as a book to represent reading time, a ball for gym class, and so on. Begin to collect these items as soon as you can. Remember to refer to students' IEPs to begin to develop a list of items and materials you will need.

▶ Start to collect menus from local restaurants. Some fast-food restaurants have picture menus that you can use as they are or that you can cut apart and place on individual index cards to make your own picture and word cards for students. Another hint—Sunday newspaper food ads provide great pictures to cut and paste for picture word cards. Be sure to laminate paper materials and picture word cards or any other appropriate items—they'll last longer. Store these items in an organized way, and put them in a place where you or your students can easily find them. Always label your storage items with picture and word labels. You may want to use the BoardMaker program by Mayer-Johnson as listed in Figure 1.5. You can also check the Wisconsin Assistive Technology Initiative website (www.wati.org) for updated technology resources and a vendor list.

Figure 1.5 Assistive Technology (AT) Vendor List

Academic/Curricular Resources	Assistive Technology (General)
Assistive Technology 7 Wells Avenue Newton, MA 02459 800-793-9227 http://www.assistivetech.com **Don Johnston Incorporated** 26799 West Commerce Drive Volo, IL 60073 800-999-4660 http://www.donjohnston.com	**Closing the Gap** http://www.closingthegap.com **CAST** Foundry Street Wakefield, MA 01880-3233 781-245-2212 http://www.cast.org **Tash** 3512 Mayland Ct. Richmond, VA 23233 800-463-5685 http://tashinc.com
Communication	**Independent Living**
AbleNet 1081 Tenth Ave. S.E. Minneapolis, MN 55414 800-322-0956 http://www.ablenetinc.com **Enabling Devices** 385 Warburton Ave Hastings-on-Hudson, NY 10706 800-832-8697 http://enablingdevices.com **Mayer-Johnson** P.O. Box 1579 Solana Beach, CA 92075 800-588-4548 http://www.mayer-johnson.com	**Independent Living Aids** 200 Robbins Lane Jericho, NY 11753 800-537-2118 http://www.independentliving.com **Sammons Preston Rolyan** 4 Sammons Court Bolingbrook, IL 60440 800-323-5547 http://www.cammonspreston.com **Rubbermaid Health Care Products** 1147 Akron Rd. Wooster, OH 44691 http://www.rubbermaid.com
Leisure Activities	**Software**
Linda J. Burkhart 6201 Candle Court Eldersburg, MD 21784 http://www.lburkhart.com **RJ Cooper & Associates** 27601 Forbes Rd., Suite 39 Laguna Niguel, CA 92677 800-752-6673 http://www.rjcooper.com	**Attainment Company** 504 Commerce Parkway PO Box 930160 Verona, WI 53593-0160 800-327-4269 http://www.attainmentcompany.com **SoftTouch Software** 4300 Stine Road, Suite 401 Bakersfield, CA 93313 877-763-8868 http://www.softtouch.com

SOURCE: Compiled by Lisa Barczyk, 2007.

Physical and Visual Arrangements Within the Room

Students with significant disabilities should spend as much time as possible with their peers in general instructional and recreational learning environments. It is likely that students with significant and multiple disabilities will spend some portion of their school day in a specially designed environment to support their unique educational needs. Typically, you will be the teacher in that classroom.

▶ When setting up your room or work areas, it is important that materials and equipment are easily accessible with adequate space for maneuverability. Materials should be labeled and stored in an organized fashion. You should also set up flexible areas around the room for different activities and for the diverse needs of the students.

▶ Diverse areas within your classroom should include the following:
   a. A table for small-group instruction
   b. An area sectioned off for quiet study area or down time that may contain a sofa, bean bag chairs, exercise ball, and rocking chair
   c. Open space for physical movement or stretching if needed
   d. An alternative to florescent lights if needed; for example, use floor lights with ceiling projection or incandescent bulbs

▶ When students are not using their wheelchairs, they should be located outside of the classroom or learning area, if possible. Designating a space in a coatroom works well. If the wheelchairs must be in the classroom due to hallway obstruction or fire codes, try not to bunch them all together. Choose several smaller, out-of-the-way areas for short periods of storage. Adaptive equipment such as standing frames, sidelyers, bean bags, floor sitters, and so on should be located in the areas where the equipment will be used by the student. If the student stands for math activities, keep the standing frame in the instructional area. If the student uses a floor sitter during the morning meeting, place the floor sitter near that area. If a wedge or bean bag is used for leisure time, locate those items in the leisure or play area.

▶ Classroom rules and expectations should always be posted. These rules should be put into simple, explicit language and include pictures to facilitate students' understanding. State the behavior that is expected or that should occur—for example, "keep your hands at your side" or "use soft voices." When posting items in the classroom, be aware of what is eye level for a student using a wheelchair.

▶ Visual displays should always include both picture and word. For example, you can use BoardMaker to create a sign with the bathroom picture paired with the word *bathroom*, to post in a spot that is easily seen by the students and teacher. Students will become familiar with the picture and word and might use this to communicate if they want to go to the bathroom and are unable to verbalize their need. Label objects in the room with pictures and words. In addition to promoting communication, this will also help students learn vocabulary and picture symbols. Labeling objects on shelves helps students to be responsible for retrieving and replacing learning materials.

Helping Administrators, General Education Teachers, and Support Staff Understand the Needs and Abilities of Students

Developing a successful relationship with your principal, fellow teachers, and support staff is very important both for you and your students with disabilities. Some administrators and general education teachers have had limited experience in working with students with significant disabilities. Because you are the best advocate for your students, a positive relationship can help smooth the way for all concerned.

▶ Special education has undergone many transformations over the years, and there might still be principals who are unaware of the latest legal and philosophical changes. It's up to special education administration and staff to help get them up-to-speed and to help them understand the continuum of services that needs to be provided. Inclusion is a process, and most school districts are now including students with disabilities in the general education classroom to varying degrees rather than keeping them in self-contained classrooms. Some principals have difficulty making the shift in thinking from the old idea of self-contained special education classrooms to inclusive general education classrooms and to using the community as a learning environment. As you assess your school situation, think about what your principal's philosophy might be. Special education administration or staff in your building might be able to help you with this. However, remember to separate fact from opinion as you listen to what they have to say.

▶ Another way to find out how your principal views special education in your school is to ask. However, don't stop him or her in the hallway for a philosophical discussion. Make an appointment, and indicate what you want to discuss when you do so. That way, your principal will be better prepared to talk with you. Also be sure to set a time at the beginning of the year—sometime before students arrive, if possible—to discuss your philosophical views and expectations of teaching with your support staff. Some of the things you may discuss with them are your role as the instructional leader, staff working as a team to support and teach students in different environments, a continuum of services, the process of inclusion over time, increase of social interactions with inclusion, allowing students to complete tasks for themselves, and documenting student progress. This might also be a good time to address any questions or concerns your support staff might have.

▶ If you are concerned about the philosophy of special education in your school and feel changes are needed, remember that you need to work along with, not against, the principal and your colleagues to help make this happen. If you are a new teacher, the best thing you can do is to demonstrate the dedication you have to your students through professionalism and commitment to your responsibilities. As you become a respected educator in the eyes of your principal and colleagues, your ability to advocate for and implement change will grow.

▶ Learn the school mission statement and philosophy. Develop a statement or some thoughts about how students with significant disabilities should be active participants in promoting the school's vision. As the teacher, consider what you can do throughout the school year to promote your personal statement or thoughts.

▶ With the general education teachers, explore inclusive learning opportunities for students without disabilities as well as students with disabilities. Some of these might include disabilities awareness programs, cooperative learning situations, lunch buddies, career exploration, and community-referenced opportunities. Provide general education teachers and support staff with a copy of your student profiles. Have open communication with administrators and other teachers and staff about students' strengths and needs. Help your fellow teachers and other staff to understand how the individual student can shine during a lesson or other times when the student is included in general education. The general education teachers and support staff should also be aware of the student's learning style and how to teach to it as well as how a student communicates and expresses him- or herself (Kluth, 2003). The following questions should be discussed with other staff in planning instruction and inclusion (Ayers, 2001; Kluth, Straut, & Biklen, 2003):

   a. Who is the student?
   b. Under what circumstances does the student thrive and succeed?
   c. What skills and abilities does this student have?
   d. What is a learning priority for this student?
   e. What is the student's awareness of him- or herself as a learner?
   f. How does the student communicate his or her needs?
   g. How can I facilitate participation in activities for this student?
   h. How can I help this student find success?
   i. What prevents me from or helps me to understand and see this student's competence?
   j. What does this student value?
   k. How and what can I learn from this student?

Discuss intervention strategies that assist in the student's success in the school community. For example, be sure to review specific behavior interventions and communication needs (see Chapter 7).

Knowing Your Community

The school building and classrooms will not be the only learning environments for your students. You must facilitate community-based or community-referenced instruction. Teaching functional skills in the settings in which they naturally occur is necessary because students with significant disabilities have difficulty with generalization (see the subsection Common Learning Characteristics in the Introduction and Overview for this book). Because of these generalization difficulties, there is no guarantee that what you teach your students in the classroom will carry over to the community setting where the skill is used. There are several things you can do to discover what your community has to offer and to facilitate instruction within the community.

▶ Familiarize yourself with your school district's policies regarding field trips into the community. There may not be a policy specifically for community instruction; however, you might be able to use the policy and procedures set up for field trips. If you cannot find this information, ask your school administrator or special education administrator. Make sure you know your school's philosophy or mission statement, the liability policy, how emergencies are handled on field trips, transportation options, policies regarding training or community instruction expenses, and staff responsibilities. In addition, it's very important to know what kind of release forms are needed, including copies of the paperwork or permission slips that must be sent home with students for a parent's or guardian's signature.

▶ Also note if the school district has an "emergency issue" policy and procedure to follow. A student who is hurt or has a medical situation could constitute an emergency issue. Make copies of the procedures to follow, and include this with community lesson plans. If nothing like this exists, you might want to talk about it with your special education administrator.

▶ See if your school district has any policies about classroom assistants and support staff going into the community to provide instruction. Discuss with administration how classroom assistants and support staff can be used to facilitate small-group, community-based, and community-referenced activities. For example, two to four students accompanied by one adult could go into the community for unobtrusive and natural instruction. Finally, the importance of providing inclusive, community-referenced instruction for students with and without disabilities should be explored and discussed (see Chapter 5, Functional Planning).

▶ Before you can plan community activities, you must explore and select appropriate settings for instruction. This can be done by considering the following questions:
   a. What environments do your students use in their daily lives with their families? Once you've compiled a short list, you will need to visit the environments you will be using. Be sure to complete the first column of the Discrepancy Analysis Form (see Figure 2.3 in Chapter 2) and determine the following about each place: When are business hours? How accessible is each business for people with disabilities? What are the times that the businesses are very busy and less busy with customers? Do they have any picture menus or other resources that might be useful for people with disabilities?
   b. What environments might students use in the future in which to live, work, and play?
   c. What businesses or instructional community settings are within walking distance of the school? Some examples could include a grocery store, shopping center, public library, or any other environment in which the student with significant disabilities can learn.
   d. Do you have public transportation from your school? What businesses are located on the bus line? Obtain public bus line schedules and maps.
   e. Does a cab company offer special rates for people with disabilities? Is there any paperwork that needs to be completed to receive a discount?

2

Organizing the Students and Their Learning Environment

One of the most important aspects of teaching for the special educator is instructional planning and meeting individual students' needs. Students with significant disabilities have a variety of issues and requirements that can challenge even the most systematic and knowledgeable teacher. This chapter is aimed at helping you organize your lessons to address IEP goals and to facilitate learning and social relationships using a variety of instructional strategies.

Chapter Outline

- The IEP and Planning
- Grouping Students
- Developing Daily and Weekly Schedules
- Individual Student Planning in a Variety of Learning Environments
- Developing Lesson Plans

■ Documenting Student Progress

■ Working With Classroom Support Staff

■ Community Experiences and Instruction

■ Advocating for Your Students and Exploring Inclusive Learning Environments

The IEP and Planning

The student's IEP is a legal document that must be addressed throughout the school year and should be kept foremost in your mind as you plan your schedule and lessons. Furthermore, as a teacher you need to continue to facilitate opportunities for students with significant disabilities to be included within general education settings and extracurricular activities to help build social relationships. Here are some ideas to help you do this.

▶ Develop an IEP-at-a-glance to make sure the student's goals and objectives are incorporated throughout his or her daily and weekly schedule (see Chapter 1, Figure 1.2, IEP-at-a-Glance). This tool will help you document and plan so that each individual student's goals and objectives are consistently being addressed.

▶ Students with significant disabilities need to be educated in a variety of environments. The special education teacher should use the IEP-at-a-glance to develop a domain list (for example, general education, domestic, community, vocational, recreation and leisure, and health and hygiene). The domain list should include specific environments if they are listed in the student's IEP. For example, the list may include environments such as a grocery store, a specific recreation location, or a specific general education class. List the students who are included under each domain or environment. Use this domain list and the IEP-at-a-glance to compare and group students with significant disabilities as you begin to develop your master schedule. But be sure to look at the objectives, as they may vary from student to student (see Figure 2.1, IEP Domain or Activity List). Be sure to make note of the special supports or adaptive material that the student might need within a specific environment or activity.

▶ Students with significant disabilities need to have meaningful involvement in the general education curriculum. The IEP goals and outcomes for students with significant disabilities should be related to grade-level standards to provide significant and active participation within the general education environment (see Figure 2.1).

▶ An ecological inventory can be a tool used to develop curriculum in domains and prioritize learning objectives for individual students with significant disabilities (Brown et al., 1979). The ecological approach is based around five areas of curriculum or domains: community, vocation, community access, recreation-leisure, and school or academics. These domains represent areas where curriculum can be developed around the skills used for day-to-day life. See Figure 2.2, Ecological Inventory, which illustrates the following steps to identify curricular content:

a. Select the domain (school, community, general education classroom, and so on).

b. Identify environments within the domain in which the student needs to learn (for example, homeroom, lunchroom, playground).

c. Select subenvironments that are a priority for the student (circle time, cafeteria line, and so on).

d. Identify activities within each subenvironment in which the student will learn and be included (listening to teacher, raising hand, choosing what to eat, washing hands, talking with friends or peers, and so on).

e. Task-analyze the priority activities into step-by-step skills. Prioritize objectives for individual student participation, and develop instructional objectives based on the student's discrepancy or needs for specific steps within the task analysis. A discrepancy analysis can be used to determine adaptations and possible instructional objectives (Brown et al., 1979). See Figure 2.3, Discrepancy Analysis Form, and also refer to Chapter 4, Curriculum, Instructional, and Assessment Planning.

▶ The COACH process (Giangreco, Cloninger, & Iverson, 2005) is an IEP planning tool that is individualized and family oriented to help prioritize outcomes within inclusive settings. *COACH: Choosing Outcomes and Accommodations for Children: A Guide to Educational Planning for Students With Disabilities* is a book that can be a resource for planning and usable forms. These prioritized outcomes can also be cross-referenced to general education standards. See Figure 2.1, bottom, Examples of Linkage Between Instructional Needs Based on the COACH and Content Standards.

Grouping Students

Students with significant disabilities should be placed in heterogeneous group ings at their home schools. However, school districts typically cluster these students at one school or at a few schools, depending on the size of the district. As a teacher of students with significant disabilities, you should advocate for your students to be placed in heterogeneous groupings. That way, supports can be provided to students who complement each other in reference to physical and behavioral needs. Individual or small-group instruction should also be provided across environments to promote the natural proportion of students with significant disabilities to students without disabilities. Here are some additional tips for grouping students.

▶ Your particular teaching situation and the number of instructional assistants assigned to you will dictate how best you can serve your students. These students are typically placed individually in general education classes with support. Other small groups of two or three students may be involved in community or small-group instruction. As the teacher, you will need to consider these models and divide your students into the smallest groups possible based upon the classroom structure and the students' needs. First, consider the students with significant disabilities who are included in general education, and provide the necessary support to them. Next, look at students who require vocational or job-training sites and community instruction. Finally, consider students who need small-group instruction. Most of your students will be in all or at least some of these models.

Figure 2.1 Example of an IEP Domain or Activity List

Lockers and Checklist	Inclusion—All	Public Transportation—
Katie	Note: See IEP-at-a-Glance	**City Bus**
Dennis	for specific objectives in	Katie
Antoine	content/subject areas.	Dennis
Michael		Antoine
Sabrina		Shannon
Shannon		
Vending Machines	**Domestic Cleaning**	**Vocational Jobs in Community**
Katie	Michael	Katie
Dennis	Shannon	Dennis
Antoine	Sabrina	Antoine
		Shannon
Shopping—Mall	**Cooking**	**Rec/Leisure—Community**
Katie	Michael	Katie
Sabrina	Sabrina	Dennis
	Shannon	Antoine
		Shannon
Shopping—Grocery Store	**Restaurant—Fast Food**	**Rec/Leisure—School**
Michael	Katie	**(Extracurricular)**
Shannon	Antoine	Katie
Sabrina	Michael	Antoine
	Shannon	Michael
		Sabrina
	Restaurant—Sit Down	
	Dennis	

Examples of Linkage Between Instruction Needs Based on the COACH and Content Standards

Instructional Goals Based on COACH	Content Standards in General Education
Makes choice when given up to four options	Demonstrates competence in general skills and strategies of reading process
Follows picture sequence to perform tasks	Demonstrates competence in general skills and strategies of reading process
Uses a calendar or schedule	Understands and applies properties of the concept of measurement
Makes purchase of merchandise or services	Uses basic procedures while performing the processes of computation
Travels safely in school and community	Understands the world in spatial terms

SOURCE: From Diane Lea Ryndak and Sandra Alper, *Curriculum and Instruction for Students With Significant Disabilities in Inclusive Settings*, 2nd edition. Boston: Allyn & Bacon. Copyright ©2003 by Pearson Education. Adapted by permission of the publisher.

Figure 2.2 Ecological Inventories for Elementary Student—Going Through Lunch Line

Domain: School

Environment: Lunch Room

Subenvironment: Lunch Line

Skill: Going through lunch line and getting lunch items

Task Analysis:

1. Stand in line.

2. Keep hands to self.

3. Follow person in front of you to lunch counter.

4. Pick up tray.

5. Grab milk from cooler.

6. Walk along counter, and wait for lunch item to be placed on tray.

7. Pick up tray.

8. Locate table that is open.

9. Walk, and sit down at table.

SOURCE: Michele Flasch Ziegler (2007).

▶ Typically, if a student requires a one-on-one instructional assistant, it is written in the IEP. As the teacher, you should make sure this support is provided throughout the day within each instructional setting. However, it is advisable to try to have multiple support staff work with each student so that he or she does not become dependent on one specific person.

▶ Consider therapists (occupational, physical, speech, mobility, and so on) as supports to provide integrated therapy and instruction to small groups. Collaborate with them, and discuss their ideas and their philosophy of integrated therapy. Remember to review their schedules, since many therapists travel to more than one school building.

▶ If you are new, don't hesitate to ask your colleagues about scheduling. Most will be glad to offer you some useful suggestions. Keep in mind that it may be a work in progress at the beginning. You may need to adjust things as time passes, so go with the flow—especially at the beginning of the school year. But as the year progresses, do your best to stick to the schedule you have created. Constant changes are confusing to your students and can exasperate the support staff with whom you work. Post your schedule in your room, and be sure to provide your administrator with a copy.

Figure 2.3 The Discrepancy Analysis Form

Person with disabilities: _____

Environment: _____

Activity: _____

I. Inventory of a Person Without Disabilities	II. Inventory of the Person With Disabilities (+/–)	III. Hypothetical Reason for the Discrepancy	IV. Solution Strategy/ Adaptation	V. Instructional Objective

SOURCE: Brown, Shiraga, York, Zanella, & Rogan (1984). Adapted with permission from L. Brown.

Developing Daily and Weekly Schedules

As the teacher, you need to develop a consistent schedule to support the learning characteristics of your students. You also need to consider and take advantage of all the supports and instructional staff that are available to them. Developing a schedule is one way to assure this will happen.

▶ Become familiar with the classroom models and the delivery models of general and special educators serving students with and without disabilities. Most important, understand how students with significant disabilities are included in general education. It is also important to know your district's policies regarding how an instructional assistant can be used within school and community settings. There may be some limitations regarding non-instructional staff, or there may be union restrictions. Check with your administrator or union representative. Also, be sure to get familiar with the daily breaks and lunch time to which your instructional assistants are entitled.

▶ Use Figure 2.4, Daily-Weekly Schedule, to begin developing a master schedule for each day of the week.
  a. Place the day at the top of the page.
  b. Next, place instructional support staff names across the top boxes.
  c. Place time of class periods for school along the left side.

▶ You should then complete the following steps to develop a master schedule for your class or students and staff (see Figure 2.5, Sample Daily Schedule).
  a. Develop IEP Domain or Activity List (see Figure 2.1).
  b. Schedule students within age-appropriate general education environments if your school does not automatically do this. Remember to consider the students' IEP goals in your scheduling.
  c. Schedule community job experience(s) or school jobs.
  d. Schedule community activities. Work with the general education teacher to provide inclusive community experience when possible.

▶ As you work on filling in the schedule for each day, list the instructional support staff or teacher, the activity, and the name of students participating in the small group.

Individual Student Planning in a Variety of Learning Environments

Students with significant disabilities learn best through routines that are familiar and that occur in a setting that makes sense to them. Academic tasks should be embedded in functional activities that have meaning for the student. For example, students can learn the math concept of 1:1 correspondence by placing a cookie in each of 10 bags for a class treat, or by distributing flyers to each staff mailbox. Students with significant disabilities will not learn to read with traditional instruction of letters and sounds of letters. By using visual cues such as pictures or drawings in a routine setting such as a morning organizational meeting, the students can learn to read their schedule for the day. When a

Figure 2.4   Daily-Weekly Schedule

Time					

Figure 2.5 Sample Daily Schedule

MONDAY

Time	Mrs. F	Ms. P	Mr. R	Mrs. T
8:00–8:15	Homeroom (rm. 27) Sam Sue Tom	Homeroom (rm. 32) Elliot Jamal	Homeroom (rm. 8) Shannon Latoya	Office/Announcements Beth and third- to fifth-grade students
Period 1 8:15–9:05	Language Arts/Reading (rm. 27) Coteach Sam, Sue, Tom ↓	Art (rm. 2) Elliot, Jamal, Latoya ↓	Science (rm. 8) Shannon, Beth ↓	(Meet Jasmine and Mom at entrance, take off coat, place in locker, and go to office.) School Job— 8:30–8:50 Collect Attendance w/peer Bathroom—8:50–9:00

Then complete a master schedule that displays the entire week for each student and instructional staff member.

Mr. R's Schedule

Time	Monday	Tuesday	Wednesday	Thursday	Friday
8:00–8:15	Homeroom (rm. 8) Shannon Latoya	→	→	→	→

SOURCE: Michele Flasch Ziegler, 2007.

model of instructional routines is used, you are able to teach functional skills that students will learn because the tasks are familiar, repetitive, and occur in natural settings. Teachers also are responsible for assuring that students' overall day and week include a variety of instructional activities with repeated practice of skills so instructional objectives can be met. Look below for some ideas.

▶ From your daily master schedule, develop individual students' schedules. Use these individual schedules to be sure your master schedule does not have discrepancies and that the instructional activities flow for each student on a day-to-day basis.

▶ Each student should have a personal schedule to help him or her develop an understanding of the day and how it flows. These schedules should be created to meet the individual needs of each student. See Figure 2.6, Examples of Visual Schedules Using BoardMaker Symbols, for ideas on how to develop a variety of schedules.

▶ It's a good idea to keep an original copy of the schedule in a place where you can access it quickly. Also provide the parents or guardians with a copy.

Developing Lesson Plans

After you have developed a master schedule, it is important to create instructional lesson plans for each activity. These plans serve as guides for instructional support staff and also document the systematic instructional cues that are needed for your students. Note that lesson plans can use different formats and structures depending on the situation and the students included in the activity. You will also need to collaborate with general education teachers to develop inclusive lessons for academic content classes (see Chapter 4, Academic Planning). The following are ways to create instructional plans for students with significant disabilities working within community or small-group instruction.

▶ Determine what type of lesson plan you will need to develop. (See lesson plan examples in Figures 2.7a and 2.7b.) Lesson plans given to instructional support staff should contain explicit information including the cues and adaptations that need to be provided. Lesson plans should also include students' individual objectives. (See Figures 2.7a and 2.7b.)

▶ After the lesson plan is developed, train support staff on the teaching procedures written in the lesson plan by verbally reviewing your plans and expectations; then allow for questions. Have your support staff observe your teaching. Then, when they are ready to take over a lesson, observe them, and offer constructive feedback. Also discuss students' learning objectives and how your students will actively participate in the lessons.

▶ Original lesson plans should be kept within an organized binder or system that you have developed. (See Chapter 1, Getting Ready.) Make sure that the instructional leader of each activity has a copy of the lesson for his or her reference during the activity.

▶ As the teacher, it is your responsibility to update lesson plans and instructional cues as your students become more independent. However, since you have developed a consistent schedule for each day of the week for small-group or community instruction, lesson plans may not need to change or be rewritten each week. (Note that this is different from collaborative lesson plans developed for inclusive academic content classes.)

Documenting Student Progress

IDEIA requires that teachers document student progress toward meeting their individual IEP goals and objectives. Section 300.309(b)(2) of IDEIA states the

Figure 2.6   Examples of Visual Schedules Using BoardMaker Symbols

Schedules can be arranged horizontally or vertically, using poster board with Velcro strips. Some students will be able to move the picture symbols to "all done" while others will simply move the symbol to an envelope when the activity is completed.

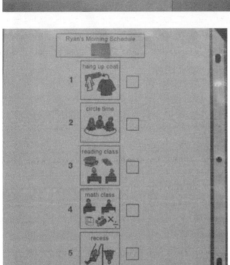

Some students will be able to place a check or other mark in the box next to the activity after it has been completed. Using page protectors and wipe off markers is a good strategy when the schedule is consistent from day to day.

The schedule below can be placed or mounted on the student's desk for easy access and use by the student.

SOURCE: Lisa Barczyk, 2007.

Figure 2.7a Sample Lesson Plan

Day _____   Instructor _____   Activity _____

Environment(s) _____   Student(s) _____

Time/Environment/ Materials	Instructional/Teaching Strategies	Student(s) Objectives/Behavior	Reinforcement/Error Correction Procedure (ECP)

Figure 2.7b Lesson Plan Example

Day ____ Monday, Lunchtime ____   Instructor __ MZ ____   Activity ___ Ordering ___

Environment(s) Fast food restaurant ____   Student(s) Tom, Joe, and Elizabeth

Time/Environment/ Materials	Instructional/Teaching Strategies	Student(s) Objectives/Behavior	Reinforcement/Error Correction Procedure (ECP)
11:00/Classroom Tom—calculator, wallet	MZ—Indirect Verbal Cue (IVC): "Tom, what do you need for going out to McDonald's for lunch?"	Tom will get his calculator and check to make sure he has his wallet and money. Given an IVC, Tom will get all his belongings for an activity 3 out of 4 consecutive trials	ECP: Wait 1 minute and repeat IVC + "Nice job remembering what you need."
Elizabeth—Dynavox and adapted wallet	MZ—Hand Elizabeth her Dynavox in her carry case, money, and picture cards for McDonald's. Direct Verbal Cue (DVC): "Put your pictures and money in your case."	Elizabeth will place her money/wallet with picture cards in her Dynavox carry case with support to hold the case open.	ECP: Gesture to items and then pocket in the case. Repeat DVC + "Way to go, Elizabeth. You are ready."
11:15/Front Lobby Joe P. from sixth grade	MZ—IVC: "Tom and Elizabeth, what should we say to Joe?"	Tom will say, "Hi, Joe"; Elizabeth will look at Joe and smile.	ECP: Gesture toward Joe, say "Hi, Joe," and wait 30 sec. for Tom/Elizabeth to respond.
11:30 Walking/Street Crossing Walk 2 blocks to McDonald's at 5th and Oakland Street.	MZ—At street intersections, IVC "What do we do at the corners?"	Tom will stop and look for traffic; Elizabeth will stop next to Joe.	"Great job, Tom—is it safe to cross?" "Good waiting, Elizabeth."

SOURCE: Michele Flasch Ziegler, 2007

following: Teachers are required to do "data-based documentation of repeated assessments of achievement at reasonable intervals, reflecting formal assessment of student progress during instruction, which should be provided to the child's parents" (http://idea.ed.gov).

▶ Documenting student progress need not be a time-consuming or difficult process. Develop a system to record student achievement that can easily be incorporated into the lesson and does not take too much time, and remember that your entire educational team should be involved in documenting students' progress across instructional environments.

▶ Refer to the IEP and the IEP-at-a-glance to plan when and in what learning environment your students will get repeated practice on instructional goals or objectives.

▶ Develop data sheets to be included with lesson plans. Remember to keep an original copy of this sheet for future use. (See sample data sheets in Figures 2.8a and 2.8b.) As you work with general education teachers, make sure the data system that is developed works for all members and does not take too much time. It's important to have ongoing communication with all team members to be sure they are implementing your system. The following website also has examples of data forms that can be used or adapted: www.newbraunfels.txed.net/admin/SpecialEd/IEP.htm.

▶ Also remember that student work samples and videotaping are authentic ways to easily document student progress. Within your weekly schedule, set a time to review and reflect on the data sheets and other forms of documenting student achievement. Make sure the method you have developed is effective and provides you with the needed information on student progress so it can be communicated with the IEP team and family members.

Working With Classroom Support Staff

Classroom support staff members assigned to work with you will have varied background knowledge and experience. Depending on your school district, their titles (e.g., classroom assistants, paraprofessionals) and educational training may vary. Classroom support staff may or may not have postsecondary education or training. IDEIA requires that instructional support staff be trained and supervised. Section 612(a)(14)(B)(iii) states that school districts must "provide paraprofessionals and assistants appropriate training and supervision, in accordance with state law, regulation, or written policy. These paraprofessionals are used to assist in the provision of special education and related services under IDEIA" (http://idea.ed.gov).

▶ Classroom support staff should receive in-service instruction from your district and should also consider taking education courses that have been developed to support learning. As the teacher, you also have a responsibility to in-service them on the overall philosophy of inclusion and of educating students with significant disabilities as well as on their day-to-day responsibilities in supporting and educating your students. Check with your building administrator or special education administrator for district training opportunities for classroom support staff. At the beginning of the year, review your own philosophical beliefs and expectations for a successful learning environment. Then share this with your

Figure 2.8a Student Progress Data Forms

Student:

Activity:

Student Objective/ Behavior	Teacher Strategies/ Cues (√)	Error Correction Procedure (ECP)	Date	Date	Date	Date	Date

COMMENTS: (Please date)

+ Independently
√ Initial Strategy
ECP—with ECP Strategy
– Did not perform skill
NC—No chance to perform
Tallies for multiple trials

Figure 2.8b Student Progress Data Forms

Activity: _____

Student: _____ Instructor: _____

Skill/Objective	Teaching Procedure/Cues	Date								

Notes/Comments:

+ Independently
√ Initial Strategy
ECP—with ECP Strategy
– Did not perform skill
NC—No chance to perform
Tallies for multiple trials

support staff. Remember to give them a chance to share their expertise and the gifts they bring to the team. Also discuss the need for all staff to implement instruction and to evaluate its effectiveness. Be sure to share each student's needs (educational or instructional support, behavioral, medical, and therapeutic) with your support staff as well as the importance of building students' independence from them, not their dependence. Stress that their role and responsibility is to ensure each student's participation or partial participation within all instructional domains—school, home, or in the community. Take advantage of naturally occurring "teachable moments" to provide issue-specific instruction and immediate feedback.

▶ Provide classroom support staff with their own schedule for each day of the week. Be sure you discuss each activity with them as well as the instructional cues that will be used and how to gradually fade these cues to meet the needs of the students with whom they will be working. When designing the classroom support staff schedule, use the format and process you used to develop your master schedule and your students' schedules. Provide a copy of staff schedules to the building administrator and anyone else who might need this information. Meet regularly with support staff to discuss student progress, decide what is going well, identify concerns, review schedules, and plan activities. Meeting time for sharing this important information should be built into the master schedule.

▶ For some students, the IEP team has determined that one-on-one (hereinafter 1:1) assistance is needed. If a student has 1:1 assistance indicated on his or her IEP, it is important to remember that it will not name a specific person. This means that it is acceptable and even necessary for the student to have different adults assisting him or her at different times. As the special education teacher, you will need to spend 1:1 time with each student to establish the best teaching strategies to use. This will enable you to train the instructional assistants to work appropriately with them. In addition, you must establish a relationship with the student as the primary instructor. Also remember that students must be able to work with a variety of people because the support persons in their life will continually change.

▶ In the instructional setting, classroom support staff should be mindful of their physical presence in relation to the student with significant disabilities. Close proximity such as sitting right next to the student or leaning over him or her for extended periods will prohibit the development of relationships and will obstruct the student's ability to engage and participate in the learning environment. Classroom support staff will need to develop and practice unobtrusive methods of providing help (Giangreco, Edelman, Luiselli, & MacFarland, 1997).

▶ The following are some responsibilities you have as a teacher toward your classroom support staff:
   a. Be sure your assistants are included in determining the amount of close-proximity instruction that is required for your students.
   b. Be sure they view you as the instructional leader in the classroom who will provide initial and ongoing training for them.
   c. Be sure to educate your assistants on basic instructional procedures and how to fade prompts. (See Chapter 3, Figure 3.1, Instructional Strategies and Fading.)

d. Be sure to include their input in instructional planning.
e. Be sure they understand that students need to be physically and interactively included within instructional settings.
f. Be sure they understand that they will be working with a variety of students—not just one specific pupil—in a variety of settings.

Community Experiences and Instruction

Community instruction needs to emphasize skills and activities that are valued, and they must be prioritized for students with significant disabilities and their parents. One important priority or outcome for these students is that they live, work, and play within an integrated community throughout their lives. In addition, they need the opportunity to access and learn within community environments to assure the generalization and transfer of skills to provide a smooth transition into adult life. The following are some helpful ideas for your consideration.

▶ Community-based instruction is defined as instruction occurring within locations or environments within the community. It can include teaching skills in numerous settings and around different goal areas such as travel, community safety, shopping, eating out, recreation/leisure, and vocation. Community-referenced instruction involves skills and objectives that are embedded within the school setting and the community. For example, some of these skills include changing clothes for gym class; washing hands; putting on and taking off coat at arrival, dismissal, and recess times; and so on. As a teacher, it's important to develop and plan for both community-based and community-referenced instruction. If you have not already done so, check with your building administrator or special educator administrator about the district policies and liability issues around transportation, staffing, and program funding and expenses for this kind of instruction.

▶ It's important to know that community instruction may need to occur as part of students' IEPs, so be sure to review each IEP to see if this is included. If it is, be sure to document each activity and the actual environment, if stated in the IEP, on the student's IEP-at-a-glance.

▶ Explore your community early on to discover what opportunities are available, and obtain the information you will need for scheduling. As stated in Chapter 1, you will want to complete an ecological inventory for the places you will be using (see Figure 2.2). Community-based instruction should occur in small groups. Peers without disabilities should be included within these groups to the greatest extent possible. (See Chapter 5, Functional Planning.) This kind of instruction should be scheduled on a consistent day and time each week. This will assure that repeated practice and ongoing instruction and documentation of learning will take place.

▶ Develop a lesson plan for each community activity, and include data collection sheets. It's helpful to develop a binder or a pocket folder for each community activity that the instructor can take along. The folder should include dividers or file folders with the following labels and information:

a. Lesson plan and data sheets
b. Copies of student emergency information, contact phone numbers, and the emergency procedures to follow as developed by the school
c. A copy of the bus schedule(s) or name and phone number of the taxi company that is used for public transportation
d. Copies of adaptive materials such as student schedules, coin cards, or picture communication boards. Students should have the original copies of these adaptive materials with them or in their desk or lockers. This will teach self-determination and build independence.

Advocating for Your Students and Exploring Inclusive Learning Environments

Teachers need to explore and understand the school and community, the curriculum, the opportunities for learning, the politics and philosophies, and the culture of the school. It is possible that you might discover that students with significant disabilities do not have the same opportunities as their peers without disabilities. Therefore, you will want to continue to explore and expand inclusive learning opportunities for your students. In order to do this, you will need to become an advocate and change agent within your school and community.

► Begin by assessing the degree to which your students are involved in the school community. Remember to consider academic, nonacademic, and extracurricular activities. Seek out opportunities for your own involvement in the school culture by coteaching, chaperoning a dance, becoming a coach or advisor for an extracurricular activity, and so on. This will help you make connections and build relationships with other students and teachers.

► Help administrators, general education teachers, and support staff understand the individual needs and abilities of your students. Facilitate the understanding that special education labels are not specific to a program or a place. Make an effort to expand the environments within your school community that will provide learning opportunities for your students and that will expand their personal relationships and increase student dignity.

► Advocate for your students and teach them self-advocacy. Teach others about inclusive education and specific disabilities. This may include working with other teachers and support staff as well as with families, PTA/PTO, and community agencies. Creating change and making a difference for your students will require you to respect and value everyone's participation. As a teacher, you must be open to new ideas and to trying different strategies for teaching and learning. Also, it is critical to be a good listener. Don't forget that students themselves can provide some of the most valuable information about teaching, learning, and relationships.

3

General Planning

Curriculum and Methods of Instruction

In the forefront of our planning for students with significant disabilities, we need to consider their unique learning characteristics. Based on these characteristics, educators must teach skills within the actual environment or setting and not in isolation. Further, students with significant disabilities require frequent opportunities to practice academic and functional skills. Let's consider what needs to take place while teaching our students academic and functional skills across settings.

Chapter Outline

- Consistency, Structure, and Routine
- Student Full and Partial Participation in the General Education Classroom
- Systematic Instruction and Fading
- Curriculum
- Blending Academic and Functional Curriculum Models

Consistency, Structure, and Routine

Consider the common learning characteristics discussed in the Introduction and Overview for this book to understand that students with significant

disabilities have difficulty generalizing and transferring skills, that they are able to comprehend less than other students, that they learn at a slower rate, and that they need repeated practice. These characteristics must drive our planning of systematic instruction across learning environments. Further, it is critical to incorporate consistency, structure, and routine into the students' week. Here are some suggestions to get you started.

▶ Develop a consistent schedule that remains the same for your students from week to week. For example, students should know they are included in the same general education classes and that they take part in the same community activities on the same days each week. These schedules should be created in a way that your students can understand (see Figure 2.6). The schedule should be reviewed with each student on a daily basis, or it might need to be reviewed more than once a day depending upon the student's individual need.

▶ Develop lesson plans that include supports and instructional cues so there is consistency among teachers and other staff. This will help facilitate clear performance expectations for the student (see Figures 2.7a and 2.7b).

▶ Be sure to include specific learning or behavior objectives within the lesson plan. These objectives must be clearly communicated to the student. Consider individual communication needs of students when delivering this information. For example, some students may need concise, shortened, verbal communication paired with written words and pictures.

Student Full and Partial Participation in the General Education Classroom

Depending on the severity of the individual's disability, the student could be present during an activity but not actively participating. Instead, the student might be sitting at a table with an instructional assistant, involved in a different activity that is skill-level appropriate. Among the reasons some students might not be involved in the general education classroom lesson are that they may not have the prerequisite skills, they cannot perform a task in its entirety, or they cannot function completely independently. However, these students should have access to age-appropriate activities to expand their participation through the concept of partial participation (Ferguson & Baumgart, 1991). Here are some ways you can do that.

▶ Think about whether or not a student can be involved in any part of an activity or if the activity can be adapted so the student can be partially involved rather than just being an observer. Consider one controlled movement that is in the student's repertoire. For example, a student could practice a controlled movement of his or her head to contact a switch attached to the wheelchair. When this movement has been perfected, it could be used to operate a computer or turn on audiovisual equipment.

▶ Rather than limiting a student's participation, build in opportunities for students to participate in everyday life activities. Use multiple modes of assessment to discover the activities that might be appropriate. For example, consider family inventories or surveys that provide information on preferences for activities and other things that the family and student are involved in on a day-to-day basis. Also consider learning objectives that have been determined by the educational team. Include the ideas of peers, coworkers, and others the student might encounter. Also consider activity-based assessments such as a discrepancy analysis. This focuses on the student's abilities and the skills needed for specific activities (see Figure 2.3).

▶ Plan your lessons in advance, and provide the needed instructional support, adaptations, and time for the student to participate. Encourage the student's participation even if he or she is not completely independent in performing the lesson activity. Any adaptations should be listed on the IEP, written in the student's profile, and should be shared with all teachers and support staff (see Figure 1.4). If you do not find this specific information, check with former teachers or support staff.

▶ Build in choice making during activities. Remember that some students do not express their preferences through conventional means. Consider using the following strategies for a student with a significant disability to make a choice:
  a. Have the student use verbalizations, vocalizations, gestures, or manual signing, or have the student look at the item of choice.
  b. Have students with limited use of their bodies use whatever physical movement they can to activate a switch or to indicate a choice between two activities or items.
  c. Watch to see if the student begins to perform the task being asked. This could indicate a choice.
  d. Allow the student to choose to stay at a task or activity for a longer time rather than having that student begin a new task.

Systematic Instruction and Fading

Principles of behavior that have proven successful in teaching a variety of skills to students with significant disabilities are applicable in all environments within the school and community (Ryndak & Alper, 2003). Further, instructional methods must be systematic and include identifying the student's learning targets or objectives and breaking them down into incremental steps (task analysis), identifying individual student needs (adaptations), and providing repeated practice of skills across environments. Moreover, strategies used by the teacher such as cueing, fading, and reinforcement must all be considered when building the student's independence.

▶ Routines should be based on a task analysis and a discrepancy analysis assessment of the student's performance in all learning environments. Then instructional strategies and adaptations can be determined.

▶ Use natural cues—e.g., the bell ringing to change classes, rather than having a peer tell student it is time to go. Try to use the least intrusive prompts, cueing, and fading procedures (see Figure 3.1). These procedures should be written into your instructional lesson plans.

▶ Plan instructional strategies and adaptations ahead of time, and provide them to students so that active participation can be achieved. Implement instructional trials across the day. This will ensure repeated practice and learning opportunities for the student. Examples of instructional trials are raising a hand to ask for help, using the bathroom, hand washing, and so forth.

▶ Make sure that students participate in a variety of instructional arrangements or groupings such as small groups, large groups, and 1:1 instruction throughout the school day.

Curriculum

As teachers, we must consider the different approaches to designing curriculum. A functional curriculum promotes the acquisition of skills

Figure 3.1 Instructional Strategies and Fading

Instructional Strategy	Definition	Fading
Verbal Prompts	Verbal prompts • Direct Verbal Cues ("Tom, stand up.") • Indirect Verbal Cue ("Tom, what do you need to do?") • Gesture (pointing, facial or physical gesture with body)	Direct Verbal Cues ↓ (fade to) Indirect Verbal Cue ↓ Physical Gesture
Modeling	A teacher or other individual demonstrates the skill or behavior, often giving verbal cues through the steps.	Model With Verbal Cue ↓ (fade to) Model With No Verbal Cue ↓ Gesture, or partial model of just a few steps
Physical Guidance *In respect to the student, also give a verbal cue, and provide hand-over-hand assistance.	The teacher physically assists the student through the activity. • Hand-Over-Hand (place hand over student's hand) • Physical Prompt (briefly touch hand) • Gestures (pointing, facial or physical gesture with body)	Hand-Over-Hand ↓ Move to wrist, elbow, and shoulder. ↓ Provide physical prompt (fade by moving out as stated above).
Time Delay	The time between the cue and instructional strategy gradually lengthens.	Increase time before providing cue or instructional strategy.
Shaping	Positive reinforcement is given to student for successful approximation of target objective or behavior. (For example, student should write first and last name on top of paper; student completes writing his or her first name.)	May add other strategies listed above, for example, time delay.

SOURCE: Michele Flasch Ziegler, 2007.

students use for everyday life or across their day such as money skills, using the bathroom, washing hands, interacting with others, and so on. The general education curriculum promotes high goals and learning for all students based upon achievement standards set by the states. These include learning targets, performance standards for grade levels, and so on. An alternative curriculum may be used for a student if he or she is unable to participate or needs 1:1 instruction for a skill or activity.

▶ As we develop curriculum for students with significant disabilities, the design should always be individualized, functional, and ecologically oriented. Decisions on curriculum should be made with families and instructional teams within our schools. The following questions should be asked to guide our instruction (Ryndak & Alper, 2003):

a. What outcomes are desired for the student?
The outcomes should be connected to the settings or environments in which the student will function while in school or during adult years. They should be similar to those of their peers. Use an ecological inventory to determine and prioritize the skills needed by your students to obtain the desired outcome (see Figure 2.2). Note that it is important to consider and discuss post-school outcomes for students with significant disabilities at a very early age. Developing communication strategies and learning functional skills will take a considerable amount of time and might need many adjustments during the school years. Planning for the student's future living, working, and recreation settings should begin in the elementary grades.

b. What skills must be learned so the outcomes can be achieved?
Skills should be considered so students with significant disabilities can live, work, and enjoy leisure opportunities within an inclusive community. This means that the skills can be performed in a variety of settings and can be understood by a variety of people.

c. How should the skills be taught and by whom?
Instructional strategies should be considered as well as systematic instruction—that is, task analyses, specific teaching strategies and instructional procedures, natural cues and corrections, reinforcement, and data collection. Decreasing the amount of verbal instruction while increasing visual and tactile cueing through repeated practice of skills in meaningful settings is most appropriate. Typically, you should first introduce new skills and plan the methods of instruction. Then, teaching assistants, related service providers, and families can practice the skill with the student in naturally occurring situations.

d. In what setting should the instruction take place?
Determine what settings within your school and community are appropriate. Also, instruction should occur at meaningful times during the day. For example, if the student is learning to remove his or her arm from a jacket, this skill should be reviewed and practiced at the natural times for taking off a coat—upon arrival at school, after recess, and upon arrival at home.

e. What skills will the student perform outside of the school setting?
If attending performances in local theaters is important to the student's family, the student will need to learn appropriate behaviors for an audience

member. This may include learning when it is permissible to vocalize, visually attending to lighted areas, or activating a switch that has been programmed with the sound of applause.

f. How will you evaluate or determine if the student has met his or her outcomes?

The IEP states how the objectives and annual goals will be evaluated. Review this, and develop a system to document the student's progress such as data collection sheets, videos, student work samples, and so on. Also, remember to communicate regularly with family members about the student's progress.

▶ As you develop curriculum, the use of natural supports, building in of choice, and autonomy are also critical. Natural supports are the relationships people have with one another that help them live a full and rewarding life. Students with significant disabilities will need to learn how to engage and interact with their classmates and with adults. Students without disabilities need to learn how to interact with students of diverse abilities. Both groups need to learn that they have common interests and unique strengths and that they can work together successfully on projects within the school and in the community.

Blending Academic and Functional Curriculum Models

Upon graduation from school, the goal for a student with significant disabilities is to live and work within an inclusive community with varying levels of support. Therefore, the development of curricula that will enable the student to function in everyday life is important. Further, the importance of having your students included in the general education classroom to support social skills and meaningful involvement is critical. Their education needs to facilitate meaningful outcomes while simultaneously promoting these students as active members of a learning community within general education (Ford, Davern, & Schnorr, 2001).

▶ IDEIA requires teachers and school districts to include students with disabilities in general education classrooms and consider academic standards when writing student IEPs.

a. Sec. 650(1)(4)(A) states that we must "maintain high academic achievement standards and clear performance goals for children with disabilities, consistent with the standards and expectations for all students in the educational system, and provide for appropriate and effective strategies and methods to ensure that all children with disabilities have the opportunity to achieve those standards and goals."

b. Sec. 654(b)(9) states that we must include "Supporting activities that ensure that teachers are able to use challenging state academic content standards and student academic achievement and functional standards, and state assessments for all children with disabilities to improve instructional practices and improve the academic achievement of children with disabilities."

▶ Blending of academic and functional skills approaches to developing curriculum is necessary. This can be done one of two ways (Ford et al., 2001).

    a. Simplify the standard so the student with a significant disability can participate in some part of the standard.

    b. Redefine the standard to represent a functional skill or priority skill for the student with a significant disability (see Figure 3.2).

▶ Consider each student's IEP goals and objectives as determined by the educational team and family. Determine where these objectives can be naturally embedded or incorporated into general education and into the student's school day.

Figure 3.2 Examples of Alternative Performance Skills Connected to State Standards

Social Studies Standard	Simplify Example	Redefine Example
Understanding of the geography of independent world in which we live—local, national, and global	• Use large map; cut out people students know and attach to areas of the map where they live or where events took place (i.e., Vacation at Disneyland). • Recognize different shapes and figures.	• State people's addresses. • Use public transportation to travel from home to school or job. • Follow school safety rules for fire alarm.
Understanding the roles, rights, and responsibilities of citizenship	• Draw or color a picture of the U.S. flag. • Match a picture of the principal to the school, mayor to the city, governor to the state, president to the country.	• Use an individualized calendar or schedule; mark off days or activities that have been completed. • Register to vote, and vote on Election Day.

English Language Arts Standard	Simplify Example	Redefine Example
Discern how written texts and accompanying illustrations connect to convey meaning.	• Place three pictures in sequence order, i.e., in order of what happened 1st, 2nd, and 3rd in the story.	• Follow a picture/word schedule of school day. • Identify women's bathroom by the posted sign.

SOURCE: Material adapted from Ford, Davern, and Schnorr (2001). Learners with significant disabilities: Curricular relevance in an era of standards-based reform. *Remedial and Special Education, 22*, 214–221. Used with permission.

4

Academic Planning

Students with significant disabilities have the right to access the general education curriculum. The special education teacher is responsible for facilitating this and for collaborating with the general education teacher and administration to provide a supportive community and meaningful curriculum for these students. An important role of the special education teacher is to develop individualized curriculum benchmarks in order to advance the consistency of learning and skill development across curricular areas and environments. This chapter provides ideas and suggestions that can help enhance your skills in this area.

Chapter Outline

- Inclusion, Least Restrictive Environment (LRE), and IDEIA

- Academic and Content Standards and Writing Individualized Education Programs (IEPs)

- Curriculum, Instructional, and Assessment Planning

- Inclusive Instructional Strategies and Adaptations

- Active Participation Versus Presence Only in the Classroom

- Collaboration and Team Planning

Inclusion, Least Restrictive Environment (LRE), and IDEIA

Students with significant disabilities should be placed in and served in the least restrictive environment, as required by section 612(a)(5) of IDEIA. Further, the use of supplementary aids and services should be used to support and educate students with disabilities "to the maximum extent appropriate" with students who are not disabled. As the special education teacher, you need to build relationships with administrators and other teachers to develop commitment to and understanding of a democratic community. Here are some suggestions to help you achieve this.

▶ Facilitate and support the involvement of your students in extracurricular activities, school groups, and grade-level field trips. Encourage social interaction and relationships among students with and without disabilities. This can be accomplished by providing students with lunch buddies; encouraging students with and without disabilities to support each other by working in pairs or small groups; or having student-led forums to discuss or share ideas, questions, or concerns. Find out what other students of the same age like to do, and create opportunities for shared experiences. You may need to help build respect and understanding on the part of students without disabilities regarding alternative and augmentative modes of communication needed by your students such as voice output technology or picture-word communication boards.

▶ Invite parents and community members to volunteer within the classroom or school or help with community projects. Facilitate discussions and sharing of ideas with other teachers and members of the school community about inclusion of students with significant disabilities and their special needs. This can be done through parent or staff in-service training, brown bag lunches, or a suggestion box.

▶ Be a reflective educator and ask questions of students, teachers, administrators, and parents to help you evaluate effective and ineffective teaching practices. Critique your lessons and collaboration strategies with other staff within your school. Reflecting on these experiences will assist you in checking your biases and assumptions as well as identifying successes.

Academic and Content Standards and Writing Individualized Education Programs (IEPs)

IDEIA states that schools must maintain high academic-achievement standards and clear performance goals for students with disabilities that are consistent with the expectation and standards of students without disabilities. Schools must also provide effective strategies and methods to ensure that all students with disabilities have the opportunity to achieve content and functional standards. Individualized education programs should be aligned with the state's academic content standards and student academic-achievement standards as well as alternate assessments. A teacher can develop

strategies to maintain standards in writing IEPs and in teaching practices for students with significant disabilities.

▶ Remember that special education is not a place but a service. Provide services and supports in the natural environments in which learning takes place. By doing this within the natural settings, you ensure that students with significant disabilities have access as well as meaningful learning opportunities.

▶ Consider the broad scope and purpose of standards. As the teacher, you must maximize the flexibility of the curriculum and create instructional opportunities for students with significant disabilities by connecting the standard to functional and individualized needs. This can be accomplished by focusing on the foundational skills within the general education curriculum (see Figure 3.2). The concept of foundational skills (Ford et al., 2001) sets educational priorities for individual students with significant disabilities.

▶ When writing the IEP, make sure the statement of present level of academic achievement and functional performance is connected to the student's current needs and future life outcomes. For example, the COACH model (see Figure 2.1) identifies the following areas to consider: communication, socialization, personal management, recreation-leisure, academics, home, school, community, and vocational (Giangreco, Cloninger, & Iverson, 2005). In addition, use a variety of assessment strategies such as surveys, observations, and student work samples to measure and document student progress.

▶ Use factual and concise information when writing IEPs. Avoid using grade-level measures as this provides no real information about the abilities and needs of your students. For example, write "the student is able to write and identify his or her name and address" rather than "the student reads at a pre-kindergarten level." Avoid using words that are not measurable such as "inappropriate," "delayed," or "weak." Describe what is observable and how often it occurs.

Curriculum, Instructional, and Assessment Planning

Both general and special education teachers can teach students with diverse needs and with significant disabilities. Good teaching begins with getting to know your students' strengths, needs, and learning styles. Next, plan instruction and assessment around these identified strengths and needs. Successful teaching and good planning can be fostered by considering the following points.

▶ Summarize assessment information for individual students. A student profile can be used to organize and synthesize this information and can then be shared with other staff and teachers who work with the student (see Figure 1.4).

▶ Choose content that is meaningful and that incorporates the general education curriculum. Design lessons up front to incorporate the needs of all learners versus adding on or making "on the spot" adaptations to lessons that have already been developed. See Figure 4.1, which can be used as an instructional tool to support this type of planning. Also consider that individual student IEP goals or objectives should be embedded within the lesson (see Figure 4.2).

▶ Design lessons to incorporate students' interest and experiences. Connect learning to real-life situations, and make content relevant to the students' lives. In addition, provide students with the opportunity to support and teach each other.

▶ Use a wide range of materials and manipulatives in your lessons. Use real items whenever possible. For instance, if you are teaching the value of money, use real coins. Also incorporate technology to enhance the content as well as the active participation of your students. The following items are online resources that can be used to provide access for reading and writing.
  a. Picture-Supported Text Resources
     News-2-You—www.news-2-you.com/index.aspx
     Symbol World—www.symbolworld.org
  b. Voice Recognition or Text to Speech
     WYNN—www.freedomscientific.com/LSG/products/wynn.asp

▶ Offer a range of assessment choices that relate to the learning outcomes, and continue to incorporate authentic approaches to assess student learning. Allow students different ways to demonstrate their understanding and learning. For example, partner or small-group assessments are good tools for assessing communication skills. A portfolio that includes samples of the student's work over a period of time can include a variety of media, including photographs or videos, art work or drawings, learning logs, projects, or role play. Data sheets are helpful to track positive changes in behavior or to document the consistency of skill performance. Video clips are helpful to assess movement, and photographs can demonstrate a skill learned over time.

Inclusive Instructional Strategies and Adaptations

You might hear teachers say that they feel unprepared or untrained to include students with significant disabilities in their classrooms, so they think they cannot effectively teach them. Since the introduction of inclusion for students with special education needs, literature in this field has included a variety of strategies and models that should be considered. Udvari-Solner (1996) presented a decision-making model for considering and creating adaptations for all students. Tomlinson (1995) discussed the differentiating instruction model that presents a variety of ways students can receive information and express what they have learned. Kluth (2003) offered the term "inclusive pedagogy," which incorporates points from each of the aforementioned models to meet the needs in a diverse classroom and community. Be sure to explore these models to further your understanding of inclusive practices. In addition, as you collaborate with general education teachers and plan lessons or units, remember to include the following to promote inclusive strategies and learning for all students.

▶ Begin by establishing a team planning format that is student-centered and determined to be an efficient method of communication. Before you discuss specific strategies or adaptations, you need to consider the configuration and demands of the general education classroom. Next, you need to compare classroom demands to individual student learning needs. Then, as the lesson plan is developed, discuss alternative methods to use during instructional time.

Figure 4.1   Instructional Planning to Meet the Needs of Diverse Learners

Class/Unit: <u>Math—Addition</u>   Teacher(s): <u>Ms. Jones</u>   Date(s): _____

Instructional Activity or Strategy	Curriculum Adaptation	Student(s) <u>Elizabeth</u>	Support Person
Addition Unit	☐ No Change Needed ☐ Positioning/Arrangement → √ Instructional Grouping → √ Cues → ☐ Pace/Time/Amount → ☐ Rules/Roles Assigned → √ Materials → (additional/special)	**Instructional/IEP Objective** Given a calculator, <u>E</u> will complete single addition problem w/90% accuracy. **List Specific Adaptations/Comments:** Opportunity to work w/partner (peer) Direct verbal cue: "The addition sign is 'plus'"; gesture to the + on the calculator. Calculator, math blocks	Mr. Smith
Instructional Activity or Strategy	**Curriculum Adaptation**	**Student(s): <u>Thomas</u>**	**Support Person**
Addition Unit	☐ No Change Needed √ Positioning/Arrangement → ☐ Instructional Grouping → ☐ Cues → √ Pace/Time/Amount → ☐ Rules/Roles Assigned → √ Materials (additional/ → special/amount	**Instructional/IEP Objective** Given more space, Thomas will show all work 100% of the time. Thomas will stay active in classroom by giving teacher eye contact and responding 2x during one class session. Sit to the front of class near the teacher. **List Specific Adaptations/Comments:** Fewer math problems (no more than 8) Larger spacing on worksheets	Mr. Smith

SOURCE: Adapted from *Wisconsin School Inclusion Project: Team Planning Packet*, 1995.

▶   Use a wide range of heterogeneous groupings throughout instruction. For example, use partners, small groups, and large groups that can be student- or teacher-directed. Groups can be based upon student interests, preferences, needs, goals, or skills. It is important to make an effort to know and understand the needs of all the learners—with and without disabilities—in the general education classrooms.

▶   Incorporate a wide range of materials within your lessons and teaching throughout the day. Toss a beach ball around the room to solicit student

Figure 4.2   Outcomes of Unit Plan With IEP Goal

Science: Plants

Unit Outcomes for Students

1. Describe the process of photosynthesis.
 	
2. Name and describe the functions of the following:
  – xylem
  – phloem
  – blade
  – epidermis
  – stomata
 	
3. Explain how plant features vary in different climates (desert, rainforest).
 	
4. Provide explanation how plant features relate to the geography and climate of region in which they are located.
	IEP Goals/Objectives:
	
	Tommy:
	
	Respond to a question by matching the picture to a correct response or written word.
	
	Interact with appropriate words and gestures to peers.
	
	Gather and organize all belongings at the end of the class period.
	
	Sue:
	
	When given 3–4 picture or word cards, a choice will be made by touching one card.
	
	Touch "help" picture or word card to ask for assistance from peer or teacher.

SOURCE: From Diane Lea Ryndak and Sandra Alper, *Curriculum and Instruction for Students With Significant Disabilities in Inclusive Settings*, 2nd edition (2003). Published by Allyn & Bacon, Boston. Copyright ©2003 by Pearson Education. Adapted by permission of the publisher.

responses; using real pictures and manipulatives during the lesson can make it come to life and increase the participation of students.

▶ Use a variety of lesson formats. Role-plays, cooperative groups, research groups, station or center teaching, and games are just a few ideas. Kagan (1989/1990) presents several different examples of cooperative groups and lesson formats that could be a helpful resource.

▶ Incorporate individual learning objectives (IEP objectives) within the lesson or activity. For example, a student may pick between two objects or pictures (chocolate or plain milk). Let the student choose the group or activity in which he or she wants to participate.

▶ As stated, a wide range of techniques should be used for summative and formative assessment. Authentic assessments facilitate student application of skills, promote higher levels of thinking through projects, provide opportunities for students to judge their own performance, and offer explicit criteria in advance.

▶ Finally, develop individual adaptations for students if the aforementioned strategies have been implemented and the student is still not an active participant in the lesson. Use the following questions, from the Udvari-Solner (1996) decision-making model, to guide you:

    a. What are the student's needs and strengths and high-priority educational goals?

    b. What environments should be used to promote achievement of goals, and are they age-appropriate and inclusive?

    c. What are the required activities and skills in the environment?

    d. How does the student perform in the environment?

    e. What are the student's performance discrepancies? (Use discrepancy analysis form/assessment.)

    f. What are priority instructional and functional objectives for the student in this environment?

Active Participation Versus Presence Only in the Classroom

Continue to challenge yourself and the general education teacher to actively involve the student with significant disabilities in the general education classroom. Many times, students are present in a classroom but not actively participating. It is critical to observe in the general education classroom to gain an understanding of expectations and of how students participate in different general education settings. Also, analyze and discuss teaching styles and how they might affect the interactions and participation of students with and without disabilities. Reflect, and continue to use the following suggestions to promote active participation.

▶ Develop a framework of instruction around the following topics that were discussed earlier in the book.

    a. Student- and family-centered activities

    b. Ecologically based assessments

    c. Functional and social relevance

    d. Systematic instruction

    e. Active participation through student initiation and choice making

▶ Every student in the general education classroom must be an informed participant who has explicit information about what is going on and about the environmental demands. The student with a disability should be given adequate support for content and social involvement, but as the teacher you must also give the student with a significant disability a meaningful way to participate and communicate socially and academically (Orelove, Sobsey, & Silberman, 2004). For example, plan key times for the student to participate using an adaptive switch to communicate, build in choice making, or give the student a role he or she can perform within a group activity.

▶ Establish and maintain opportunities for learning and social interactions between students with and without disabilities. This can be done by fostering interdependence as well as independence.

▶ Analyze and change the level of abstract information, or increase the degree of complexity of context.

▶ Connect information to the student's current knowledge and experiences. This will increase learning that is age appropriate and relevant to present and future life expectations.

Collaboration and Team Planning

As lessons are developed that include appropriate and inclusive strategies, all teachers, administrators, parents, and other school support staff must understand the importance of collaboration and cooperation. This can be a challenging goal. Listed below are a few principles of collaboration that should be considered.

▶ Develop a common mission to provide responsive instruction and learning for all students. Everyone must share the same vision of inclusion, planning, and instruction, and the belief that all students can learn.

▶ Teachers must share roles and responsibilities within the inclusive classroom that incorporate shared accountability for all students. Take turns teaching and supporting the class as a whole in addition to supporting individual students. Look further into your school community to find ways for everyone to be involved in the teaching and learning process. For example, the lunchroom staff can support students as they move through the lunch line and make food choices.

▶ All team members should share in leadership roles and in other responsibilities such as leading team or IEP meetings, calling the families, completing paperwork, and so forth. Alternate tasks so that no one is overburdened. Successful collaboration requires time to meet face-to-face to develop whole-class lessons for all students. Work with your administrator, and ask for a common planning time, preparation period, or time before or after school. See Figure 4.3 for ideas and other strategies that can be used for collaboration.

Figure 4.3   Ideas for Common Planning and Collaboration Time

IDEA	EXPLANATION
Team Meetings	Teachers and support staff can meet as often as needed (once per week, twice a month, and so on). A time should be selected when teachers can meet together—for example, before school every third Wednesday of the month.
Lunch or Breakfast Meetings	Plan a meeting around a mealtime together. This time could be used for planning, brainstorming, or sharing successes and difficult situations.
"Quick Contact" Meeting or "Just Touching Base"	This may be a time determined by two teachers to touch base weekly to make sure everything is running smoothly or to decide if something needs to be changed for the next week. Teachers might discuss students, curriculum, or instructional or adaptations issues.
Written Dialogue or Communication Forms	Some teachers develop a form that can be completed quickly and placed in a colleague's mailbox or passed around to all team members. Ideas and concerns can be shared this way.
E-mail	This can expand written dialogue between colleagues. Lesson plan ideas and coplanning can also be done by e-mail.
Information Binders	Teachers may keep a binder with student information and schedules, unit plans, lesson plans, and any other pertinent information—for example, student medical information. This binder should be located where it can be accessed by all teachers and team members.

SOURCE: From Paula Kluth, *You're Going to Love This Kid! Teaching Students With Autism in the Inclusive Classroom* (2003). Published by Paul H. Brookes Publishing Co., Inc., Baltimore, MD. Copyright ©2006. Reprinted by permission of the publisher.

5

Functional Planning

For their students with significant disabilities, teachers must provide meaningful curriculum that will enable them to live, work, and play within the communities in which they live. IDEIA states that we must consider the academic, developmental, and functional needs of students with disabilities. Functional outcomes for students can be promoted through carefully considering the skills needed in life, independent and daily living, recreation and leisure, community mobility, work experience, vocational settings, career development, and postsecondary education. These skills can be taught and used in the natural environments through community-based instruction or embedded within the general education instruction through community-referenced learning (see Figure 5.1). Consider the following points to plan and teach meaningful functional skills to students with significant disabilities.

Chapter Outline

- Planning for Community and Functional Skills Instruction
- Functional Learning Outcomes
- Functional Instruction
- Inclusive Examples
- Social Skills and Peer Relationships
- Self-Advocacy and Self-Determination
- Transition and Outcomes

Planning for Community and Functional Skills Instruction

Because community instruction is part of the student's Individualized Education Program (IEP), school systems are responsible for the students when they leave the school grounds. Teachers will need to work with the building administrator to make sure that policies and procedures are followed before beginning instruction within community settings. Obtain or develop the following information before beginning this instruction.

▶ Learn your school and district's policies concerning the issue of liability and especially who is responsible if a student is injured while out in the community. Liability refers to who is accountable if someone is injured while in the community or if property is damaged due to negligence. For example, if a teacher or staff person is not providing supervision, this could be construed as negligent behavior. Typically, community instruction is covered under the same policies as field trips.

▶ Develop a manual that defines policies and procedures, including plans for training and instruction of all teachers, school staff, and support staff. Emergency procedures should also be included in the handbook.

▶ Consider transportation options. Transportation can sometimes be seen as a barrier. However, the following choices should be evaluated:
   a. Walking
   b. Public transportation such as buses or taxis
   c. Transportation provided by agencies
   d. School buses
   e. School van or driver education vehicles
   f. Private vehicles

For some students, learning how to use transportation options in their community will be part of the IEP goals or transition planning activities. In addition, it's important for student to learn how to manage behavior while on public transportation.

▶ Consider the following options for program funding or expenses:
   a. Involve students in activities or environments that do not require money such as the library, mall walking and window shopping, community centers, community parks, and recreation centers.
   b. Involve students in activities that require little money but can incorporate numerous skills such as using a vending machine to practice money recognition and value, fine motor skills, choice making, and drinking or eating skills.
   c. Ask families to send money for students to purchase items for home, so they can practice this skill.
   d. Convert a part of the classroom budget to funds that can be used for community instruction, or ask school administrators to set up a separate budget.
   e. Conduct fundraisers. Sell items such as baked goods, pizza, school spirit buttons, and so forth, or operate a school store.
   f. Offer a service to other staff members in the school. Staff members could provide a shopping list and money for students to make purchases at the store, staff members can provide clothing that requires a trip to a nearby dry cleaner, and so on.

▶ Work with your building administrator and other teachers to creatively schedule time (block schedule, specific class period of the day) in which community instruction can be provided with minor loss of academic instructional time. For example, two teachers could work together to provide students a study hall time in which to complete homework or do independent reading. During this time, a small group of other students could go to a store to purchase materials to be used for a project. Functional skills would be incorporated into the lesson plan. See Inclusive Examples later in this chapter.

Functional Learning Outcomes

IDEIA (sec. 300.600[b][1]) requires that there be "improved educational results and functional outcomes for all students with disabilities." As a teacher, you can assess meaningful skills through a functional skills approach. This approach can be used to prioritize age-appropriate individual skills that students must learn in order to gain increased independence. This should be written into the student's IEP, including the postsecondary transition plan. The following points should be incorporated into your planning to facilitate functional outcomes for students with significant disabilities.

▶ Teachers are required to provide a statement of present level of performance and measurable annual goals in the IEP that include the academic and functional needs of the student with a disability. Also, the part of the IEP related to transition services (beginning no later than the first IEP to be in effect at the age of 16, or younger if appropriate) must include measurable postsecondary goals related to training, education, employment, and independent living skills when appropriate.

▶ Use age-appropriate functional assessments to prioritize skills that should be practiced. A task analysis and ecological inventory are two assessment tools that should be used (see Figures 2.2 and 2.3).

▶ Along with the assessment information obtained, functional skills should be prioritized based upon student needs and wants as well as on input from family and friends. In Chapter 1, Getting Ready, helpful methods are suggested for gathering information about the student's priorities from family and other people involved. These include family inventories, COACH, and the MAPS process.

▶ Because functional skills are specifically used in natural environments, family members and friends can also provide repeated practice for these skills outside of the school day. Collaborate with families, and provide them with clear information about instructional procedures used at school so that reinforcement can occur outside of the school day. During school, use settings that are frequented by the student and his or her family or friends if at all possible. Moreover, natural supports can be built within these community environments if students are provided consistent times and days that they practice or build functional outcomes. The natural support approach uses the people and things that are normally in the environment and can provide help to the student. Examples of natural supports are peers, neighbors, family members, coworkers, and so on.

▶ When prioritizing skills or outcomes for transition-age students, consider realistic supports and services that can be maintained after graduation from high school through accessing community agencies or other natural supports.

Functional Instruction

Community-referenced instruction addresses functional outcomes that may be needed for inclusion and can be taught within the general education environment—for example, responding to questions, raising a hand, and following directions. Community-based instruction addresses additional learning outcomes for inclusion within community settings such as eating with utensils, purchasing items from a grocery store, placing a food order at a fast food restaurant, or calling a friend (see Figure 5.1). Some functional skills will cross both school and community settings such as making a choice, telling time, and so on. These skills should be taught in the community or natural settings in which they are used. See Figure 5.2 for ideas regarding embedded functional skills taught within the school day. Consider the grade-level factor for students with significant disabilities.

▶ Students of all ages should access community settings and should be provided instruction on functional skills. The functional activities and skills in which students are engaged should always be age appropriate throughout the school years.

▶ During the elementary years, teachers should focus on community-referenced instruction—for example, getting on a bus, waiting in line, or picking lunch food items. Students should be provided with the opportunity to increase proximity and interactions with peers that are not disabled. Even though providing instruction in school settings does not guarantee the students will perform the skill in the community when they get older, it does provide a natural opportunity for interaction with peers without disabilities. See section on Inclusive Examples in this chapter for inclusive scenarios of community instruction.

▶ During the middle school years, students with significant disabilities will continue to get community-referenced instruction in the general education environment but should increase community-based instruction and career awareness. If possible, begin providing students with some job experience or training near the end of middle school. Also, focus on the community environments used by the student and his or her family. Note that many age-appropriate skills are difficult to practice without going into the community. Purchasing and using personal hygiene care items is a good example. Many skills can be discussed in school; however, the goal is to provide instruction in the actual environment in which the skills are used.

▶ In high school, community instruction should intensify. Functional skills should be built upon what the student has learned during elementary and middle school years. Furthermore, transition outcomes and goals should be considered, and instruction should be built around these outcomes so that students with significant disabilities can be as independent as possible upon graduation from school. Curriculum choices should be based upon students' adult life goals. Some students may focus on advanced academics, and others may focus on job training or a vocational trade.

▶ Transition planning within IDEIA requires that planning occur and include a coordinated set of activities in the areas of training, education, employment, and independent living skills (when appropriate).

Figure 5.1   Community-Based Instruction (CBI) and Community-Referenced Instruction (CRI)

Skill: Dressing

CBI   Putting on coat to go to work
        Taking off coat when arriving at work

CRI   Putting on coat to go out to recess
        Taking off coat when returning to school
        Changing clothes for gym class

Skill: Purchasing

CBI   Going to the grocery store; picking out food items; paying for them
        Purchasing a soda at a fast food restaurant
        Paying for a movie

CRI   Paying for lunch in the cafeteria
        Purchasing a pencil from the school store
        Using a vending machine from the school lobby
        Purchasing a ticket for an athletic event

Skill: Communicating Using Picture or Word Symbols

CBI   Locating items at the grocery store from a picture list
        Indicating desired food at a fast food restaurant by choosing the picture card
        Ordering food item by using a picture card and written comments
        Asking where the bathroom is by using a bathroom picture or word card

CRI   Using a picture schedule throughout the school day
        Choosing hot or cold lunch using a picture card
        Indicating the temperature by choosing the picture that correlates with the weather
        Choosing an activity based on two items or pictures presented
        Ordering a snack by choosing a picture from a concession stand

---

SOURCE: Adapted from P. Wehman and J. Kregel, *Functional Curriculum for Elementary, Middle, and Secondary Age Students With Special Needs* (2nd ed.), 2004, Austin, TX: PRO-ED. Copyright ©2004 by PRO-ED. Adapted with permission.

Inclusive Examples

Consider the following strategies and scenarios to plan and provide community experiences that include students with and without disabilities.

▶   Community and functional skills instruction can be incorporated into service learning projects, project-based instruction, or community research teams. Service learning incorporates meaningful volunteer work that is connected to learning objectives. Such service could include painting a youth center, cleaning a park or school yard, organizing a reading fair, or starting a recycling program. Project-based instruction connects an artifact or finished project to learning objectives of a lesson or unit. Examples might be producing a movie or video,

Figure 5.2 Embedded Functional Skills Within the Elementary School Day

	Employment	Independent Living	Recreation/Leisure	Community
Reading	Reading books on careers or jobs Looking at pictures of and discussing jobs	Reading a written daily schedule or using pictures	Looking at ads or catalogs to determine desired toys	Comprehending community signs
Writing	Writing name or affixing label on school work, art projects, sign-up charts, etc.	Listing foods from 4 food groups that make a nourishing meal	Signing in at an after-school club E-mailing or instant messaging a friend	Signing out in the office when leaving school early
Listening	Listening to directions	Listening to the weather to determine what to wear	Listening to music or a book on tape	Listening to a guest speaker or a leader on a field trip
Communication	Asking for help	Indicating hot or cold lunch	Choosing an activity at recess	Asking where bathroom is located
Math	Using a calculator	Weighing a produce item at the grocery store	Paying for lunch Understanding the value of money	Navigating around school or community
Problem Solving/ Survival Skills	Performing a classroom job	Understanding meaning and use of "9-1-1"	Understanding and following rules of a game	Walking in the crosswalk
Personal/Social	Working with a classmate to complete task or assignment	Taking a bath 3–5 times a week	Inviting a friend over after school	Choosing a free-time activity

Embedded Functional Skills Within the Middle to High School Day

	Employment	Independent Living	Recreation/Leisure	Community
Reading	Reading the classifieds for a job	Comprehending direction on medication	Checking a movie time in the newspaper	Reading a bus schedule/knowing a landmark for a bus stop
Writing	Filling out a job application	Planning a balanced meal; making a grocery list	E-mailing or instant messaging a friend	Writing and leaving a note for your parent /guardian
Listening	Listening to a boss explain your job	Listening to bells and attending next class	Listening to music or books on tape	Using eye contact when someone is talking with you
Communication	Asking for a day off or calling the school office when you are sick	Telling someone your daily schedule	Asking someone to go out on a date	Correctly letting a taxi driver know where you are going

	Employment	Independent Living	Recreation/Leisure	Community
Math	Understanding how to save money you have earned	Measuring for a recipe	Telling time and getting to the place when the activity starts	Determining how much money is needed or if you have enough money for an outing
Problem Solving/ Survival Skills	Settling a disagreement with a friend/coworker	Having a system to take medication at correct time/day	Choosing an alternate plan if there is bad weather and you cannot do the activity you planned	Knowing what to do if your ride does not show up on time
Personal/Social	Taking a break with a coworker	Making an appointment with a doctor	Calling a friend to go to a movie	Joining a school club or health club

SOURCE: From Paul Wehman, *Life Beyond the Classroom: Transition Strategies for Young People With Disabilities* (4th ed.), Baltimore: Paul H. Brookes Publishing Co. Inc. Copyright ©2006 Paul Brookes. Reprinted by permission of the publisher.

designing a brochure or school newspaper, or creating a board game. Research is a way for all students to get involved and obtain information in varied formats. Students can work in groups and go right to the source to interview, observe, and obtain information or artifacts. This type of instruction lends itself to including students with diverse abilities.

► Consider this example of an inclusive community experience to give you an idea of what is possible. A teaching team—two educators, one responsible for special education and the other for general education—planned part of the third-grade social studies curriculum. They were able to involve students with and without disabilities in scheduled community outings to the local grocery store. The special education teacher worked with a small group of third-grade students with and without disabilities to plan a weekly project; group participants varied each week. A cooking or snack activity was selected based on the curriculum content for the week. Using assistive technology as needed, students developed a shopping list and created a set of sequenced directions to complete the project. Because one social studies session each week was a free read time, the small group could walk to the grocery store and purchase the items on the list. Each student worked on individual learning objectives. For example, the student with a significant disability located two items in the store that were on a picture list; other students worked on concepts such as estimation, calculation, and money skills. As the culminating activity, the small group then taught the other students in the class about the project. The general and special education teachers circulated as the small groups of students were teaching to offer assistance as needed. Overall, students with and without disabilities were working together on academic standards, social relationships, and communication skills in the context of a social studies class with an option for inclusive community–based instruction.

▶ Awareness of a school's practices related to its mission can create opportunities for community-based instruction. A middle school rewarded two students each week with a lunch at a local fast food restaurant for good deeds or acts of service during the previous week. The special education teacher arranged for a student with significant disabilities to join the other students and school staff representative on the lunch outing. This student was able to work on functional IEP objectives such as how to greet strangers, how to socialize, and how to order lunch.

▶ Block scheduling or interdisciplinary teaching is used at some high schools to provide longer periods of instruction in particular subject areas. During a social studies and language arts block, students with and without disabilities were included in the classroom. The teacher incorporated research- and project-based instruction in her teaching at a rural high school. Students used a distance video to discuss topics and ideas with students in an urban high school of diverse cultural and ethnic backgrounds. For example, two students attending the urban high school lived in Africa. Interviewing took place through distance video conferencing. Students from one class asked the two students questions about what their life was like in Africa and how it differed from the United States. Students from both high schools were able to learn about each others' culture and life. The students with disabilities were included and able to share their experiences.

▶ A high school teacher coordinated a community-referenced instruction as well as a community-based experience with each lesson or unit being taught (see Figure 5.1). Students went into the community to research and learn about the topics of study—an example of this would be the historical relevance of buildings and their architecture. The research was done through interviews, video-taping, or observation. With each lesson, the objectives for students would be differentiated to meet individual students' needs. Students with significant disabilities most likely had repeated practice on a single objective. The teacher obtained and documented individual student progress toward the objective connected to the IEP as it related to the role or responsibility the student had in the small-group research project—for example, interviewing related to communication skills, documenting observations related to accessing a computer, turning a video camera off and on related to using a switch.

Social Skills and Peer Relationships

Students experience success in school when they develop friendships and spend time with friends. For students with significant disabilities, developing these friendships is difficult if they are educated in self-contained classrooms with minimal contact with peers without disabilities. As teachers, we must continue to build a school community that embraces relationships and facilitates social interactions between diverse students in school and in life outside of school.

▶ Students must respect each other. Promote acceptance and belonging by allowing students to share things about themselves, and learn about differences among them. As educators, we must demonstrate through our interactions and our teaching that we value and respect differences. Teachers can also provide activities that build community through icebreakers, interviews, and working together to provide a service.

▶ Teach and facilitate communication among students. Students with significant disabilities do not always use conventional means of communication. Some might need alternative communication systems. Facilitate interactions among students by teaching individual students conversation strategies and modeling these techniques within your teaching.

▶ Use different grouping strategies within your classrooms and school to help students learn about each other and from each other. Students can work with a partner or a group of three or four students in different activities or projects to accomplish a goal or to support each other in finishing a task. Another way this can be accomplished is through cross-age tutoring or the reading buddies program.

▶ Using different lesson formats can also promote interaction and interdependence. Through group discussions, games, and cooperative learning, students will interact and develop social relationships.

▶ Support and facilitate opportunities for students with significant disabilities to build social relationships and natural supports outside of school. Provide support and help students with disabilities to get involved in extracurricular activities or school organizations such as sports clubs, student council, 4-H groups, school dances, fundraisers, and so forth.

Self-Advocacy and Self-Determination

Teachers must promote self-determination to facilitate best practices. Students that display this trait have behaviors that enable them to achieve desired goals or outcomes and to enhance their quality of life. Self-determined behaviors include choice making, decision making, problem solving, goal setting and goal attainment, self-advocacy, self-awareness and efficacy, and outcome expectancy. As teachers, we can model and facilitate these behaviors using a number of methods.

▶ The following concepts or ideas should be incorporated into the curriculum.
  a. Making choices (choice, accomplishments)
  b. Achieving success (setting goals)
  c. Persisting (problem solving, advocating, leadership)
  d. Adapting to the environment (efficacy)
  e. Building social networks for success (supports)

▶ Research and review possible curricula that have been developed to teach self-determination or self-advocacy behaviors (Wehman, 2006):
  a. The ChoiceMaker materials from Sopris West Educational Services (http://store.cambiumlearning.com/InitialSearchResults.aspx?search type=Basic&sorttype=Basic&Query=ChoiceMaker&criteria)
  b. Whose Future Is It Anyway? Self-determination curriculum developed by Dr. Michael Wehmeyer. Contact the Beach Center on Disability (www.beach center.org/education_and_training/self-determination.aspx)

    c. The Next S.T.E.P. Program. Contact Pro-Ed Publishing (www.proedinc .com/customer/ProductLists .aspx?SearchWord =The%20Next%20S.T.E.P.)

    d. The Self-Advocacy Strategy materials from Edge Enterprises, Lawrence, Kansas (www.kucrl.org/sim/strategies/advocacy.shtml)

    e. TAKE CHARGE for the Future. Contact Oregon Health Sciences University Center on Self-Determination (www.ohsu.edu/searchresults/controller.jsp? Ntt=TAKE+CHARGE+ for+the+Future&Ntk=All&sid=11A8371260C0)

▶ The following strategies can be used to teach self-determination skills to students with significant disabilities within the general education classroom or within community settings.

    a. Build choice making within daily instruction and lesson plans. Examples include picking hot or cold lunch, deciding in which activity to participate, making a choice to demonstrate learning such as drawing a picture, taking a test, or doing a project, and so on.

    b. Student-directed learning involves students setting behavior or learning goals. Then they are taught to self-monitor and to evaluate their progress via a checklist with tasks that need to be accomplished or with behaviors that need to be displayed. Students check off each item on the list when they are done.

    c. Problem solving involves students needing to find solutions to a problem in school or in the community. Systematic instruction can be used to teach problem solving including having students think aloud, discuss possible steps toward a solution to a particular problem, and consider the possible supports or materials needed.

▶ Self-determination should be incorporated into the life span of learning for every student. More complex self-determination strategies can be used as students get older and begin to set transition goals for their life after school. Train students and work with them to lead their own IEP and transition meetings. A guide to student-led IEPs is available online at http://www.nichcy.org/stuguid.asp.

Transition and Outcomes

Transition is a life-long process and is not just the responsibility of the secondary-level teacher or transition teacher. As educators of students with significant disabilities, we must continue to provide repeated practice and build independence throughout our students' lives.

▶ Many functional skills are embedded throughout the curriculum and school day. Consciously take the time within your lesson plan and teaching to add functional learning objectives. For example, at circle time in a kindergarten classroom during a discussion of the weather, actively engage your students, and allow them to choose from pictures the appropriate clothing to wear based on the day's weather.

▶ Transition skills should be developed beginning with the early school years for students with significant disabilities. For example, elementary-age students should learn about careers and school jobs; in middle school students should begin to explore careers through job shadowing and other experiences. Then, in high school, students should continue to increase job experiences and awareness of requirements for specific career paths.

▶ Actively involve parents, significant family members, and students in educational decisions. Work with them to determine preferences, interests, and educational goals. Collaborate on increasing the student's active involvement in school and community activities such as the YMCA, church groups, volunteering, and so on.

6

Using Assistive Technology as a Learning Support

IEP teams are required to consider whether or not a student with a disability needs assistive technology to benefit from his or her special education program. When teams decide upon and review IEP goals and objectives, it is important to think about the tools and devices that may be available to assist the student in making progress toward these goals.

Chapter Outline

- Definition of Assistive Technology (AT)
- The SETT Framework
- Use of Assistive Technology for Communication
- Use of Assistive Technology to Access Literacy
- Use of Assistive Technology to Control the Environment
- Use of Assistive Technology to Hold Things
- Use of Assistive Technology to See Better

■ Use of Assistive Technology to Hear Better

■ Use of Assistive Technology for Computer Access

■ Use of Assistive Technology for Eating or Dressing

■ Use of Assistive Technology for Access to Recreation and Leisure

■ Documenting Assistive Technology in the IEP

Definition of Assistive Technology (AT)

To begin this chapter, a definition of assistive technology is provided to ensure a clear understanding of the scope of this term. Assistive technology is defined by IDEIA 2004 as "any item, piece of equipment, or product system, whether acquired commercially off the shelf, modified, or customized, that is used to increase, maintain, or improve functional capabilities of a child with a disability." Assistive technology defines a broad range of devices including low-tech items such as pencil grips, simple switches, and built-up handles; mid-tech devices such as programmable voice output communication devices; and high-tech mechanisms including computers, software programs, and adapted keyboards. These devices can be used for purposes such as communication, learning, physical access, and active participation. Most states have assistive technology resource centers or lending libraries that provide teachers the opportunity to try many of the high-tech products before purchasing them. Check with your school district to determine how assistive technology devices are obtained for trial or purchase.

The SETT Framework

The SETT Framework, developed by Joy Zabala, is an organizational tool used by many teams across the country to gather and organize information about the Student, Environment, Tasks, and Tools so that common decisions can be made in regard to the need for assistive technology solutions. The SETT Framework includes participation from the student, parent, teacher, therapists, instructional assistants, and any other pertinent stakeholders.

▶ Student Considerations—Team members must consider the following questions and include the student in the decision making whenever possible:
   a. What does the student need to do that he or she cannot do independently right now?
   b. What are the student's current abilities and special needs related to the areas of concern?
   c. What are the student's interests and preferences?

▶ Environmental Considerations—The team should consider all environments in which the student participates with regard to
   a. Arrangement (instructional and physical),
   b. Support (available to both the student and the staff),

  c. Materials and equipment (commonly used by others in each environment),

  d. Access issues (technological, physical, instructional), and

  e. Attitudes and expectations (staff, family, other).

▶ **T**ask Considerations—The team should examine the specific tasks in which the student is involved during his or her daily life, including the most critical elements of each task.

  a. Consider the specific tasks that occur in the student's natural environments that enable progress toward mastery of IEP goals and objectives.

  b. Determine what specific tasks are required for active involvement in the identified environments (related to communication, instruction, participation, productivity, environmental control).

▶ **T**ool Considerations—In the SETT Framework, tools are the devices, services, strategies, training, accommodations, and modifications—anything that is needed to help the student succeed. When considering the tools that would be helpful, the team should think about ones that the student can use across environments. After analyzing data collected in the Student, Environment, and Task sections, and when it has been determined that the student requires assistive technology devices or services to make progress toward educational goals, the team is ready to engage in the following activities:

  a. Brainstorm specific tools that could be included in a system to address student needs.

  b. Select the most promising tools for trials in the natural environments.

  c. Plan the specifics of the trial (expected changes, when or how tools will be used, cues, and so on).

  d. Collect data on effectiveness of the chosen tools.

For additional information on using the SETT Framework, please refer to the 2005 article by Joy Zabala, "Using the SETT Framework to Level the Learning Field for Students With Disabilities" (see References), or go to Joy Zabala's website at http://sweb.uky.edu/~jszaba0/JoyZabala.html.

Use of Assistive Technology for Communication

Augmentative and alternative communication is a term used to describe items that are used to help a person communicate when [his or her] spoken communication is not effective. There are many items and devices that can be used to help increase or "augment" a person's ability to communicate. These include pictures, symbols, and printed words. They may simply be printed on pieces of paper or cardboard or used on a computer or special dedicated device.

Penny Reed and Elizabeth Lahm (2005)

▶ For students with significant disabilities, effective communication interventions or devices are critical to the student's ability to actively participate in community and inclusive school settings. The speech and language pathologist at your school is the best resource for augmentative and alternative communication.

Even if students do not receive direct speech therapy services, the therapist can be of assistance in providing examples of augmentative and alternative communication devices, catalogs, and district-level resources.

▶ The following are some examples of augmentative communication devices:
   a. Communication boards—Even when voice output devices are being used by the student, having a portable, easy-to-use communication board is a valuable backup if the higher-level technology needs repair or reprogramming. Students should always have some method of communication available to them.
   b. Book with pictures, objects, letters, and words—Always pair the picture with the word for students with significant disabilities. Using a binder with plastic inserts or a photo album to organize pictures of common objects or the student's preferred choices are easy-to-use communication methods.
   c. Simple voice output device (e.g., BIGmack)—These devices typically can record one message for a specified amount of time. It is suggested that the recordings be made by a same-sex peer so that the voice is the same age and sex of the student using the device. Attaching a picture symbol or small object to the top of the device assists the student in recognizing what he or she will say. Voice output devices work like switches and are activated by depressing a large button.
   d. Voice output device with levels (e.g., Step-by-Step)—This device allows up to 75 seconds of recording time and holds the number of messages that can be recorded within the time limit. This is useful for reading books, following a recipe, or using a variety of greetings. For example, instead of using a simple voice output device to say "hello" each time, this device allows programming for "hello," "hi," "how are you," "have a nice day," and so forth, so that a different message in the same general category is expressed when the device is activated.

▶ Picture symbols are frequently used to help students with significant disabilities to communicate, learn, and organize. The BoardMaker software program from Mayer-Johnson has a library of 4,500 picture symbols and the ability to add digital pictures to the library for greater personalization. To promote age-appropriate communication and activities as students get older, it is important to use pictures of actual objects rather than picture representations.

Use of Assistive Technology to Access Literacy

For students who cannot hold a book or turn the pages, assistive technology tools and solutions will help them participate in reading activities. Some examples are listed below; refer to Figures 1.5 and 6.1 for purchasing information. These strategies will help you incorporate reading and literacy skills throughout the school day.

▶ The following are some useful low-tech solutions:
   a. Adapt the pages of classroom books with extra-large paper clips, small clothespins, or other tactile materials that will make the pages easier to turn.

      b. Use a slantboard, book holder, or a 3- or 4-inch ring binder to prop up a book for easier viewing.

      c. Adapt magazines with simplified text or picture symbols. Placing magazine pages in heavy-duty page protectors inside a three-ring binder gives weight to the paper and helps pages stay flat.

      d. Make a book from a poem by using one line per page and adding pictures and picture symbols.

▶ The following are some mid-tech solutions:

      a. Record books onto a Step-by-Step communicator (vendor is AbleNet) for single-switch reading. This is especially helpful when students are taking turns reading a book or when an older student with significant disabilities is "reading" a book to younger students. This is a great opportunity for ongoing service learning experiences in which students with disabilities engage in activities that help others while also developing their own skills.

      b. Make a book for the classroom using picture symbols, digital pictures, and repeating lines. Repeating lines, such as "At the zoo I saw . . ." can be recorded on a simple voice output switch (such as a BIGmack) so that students can read that portion of the story while practicing switch activation on each page.

      c. Use picture symbols pertinent to the story or subject matter to create a communication board so that the student can ask questions or make comments.

▶ The following are some high-tech solutions:

      a. Use PowerPoint (Microsoft Office) to develop electronic books that can be burned to CDs. Single-switch software will allow students to "turn" pages by activating the switch.

      b. Record books into a BookWorm (vendor is AbleNet) for easier access by students.

      c. Access books online, such as adapted text from www.readinga-z.com.

Use of Assistive Technology to Control the Environment

Environmental controls are those devices that remove the physical barriers to a student's ability to access the living and learning environments. There are several categories of environmental controls including switches, electrical control units, and battery control units or adaptors. (See the resource list in Figure 6.1.)

▶ Switches turn things on and off. They connect to appliances, toys, games, and portable music that have been set up to receive an auxiliary switch. When the switch is activated, the toy or device will operate; when contact is removed, the device will stop. There are many types of switches, and the selection of which switch to use depends on the individual needs and abilities of the student. The most commonly used switch is the pressure switch that requires the student to touch the switch and apply pressure (amount can vary) to activate it. Picture(s) paired with word cards should also be placed onto the switch so the student knows what the switch is operating. Picture-word cards can easily be changed by using Velcro to adhere the cards to the switch. Wireless switches are also available

Figure 6.1 Assistive Technology Resources for Teachers

Online Resources:

News-2-You   *www.news-2-you.com*

Subscription required. Downloadable weekly newspaper with theme-related adapted text, jokes, recipes, and more. This newspaper generally follows the school year calendar from September to mid-June.

Reading A to Z   *www.readinga-z.com*

Subscription required after free trial. This website has more than 1,500 downloadable leveled (developmentally appropriate) books that are professionally written. Lesson plans are also available.

Manufacturers/Products:

AbleNet   *www.ablenetinc.com*

Good resource for switches, voice output communication devices, and other assistive technology products. Produces the BIGmack, Step-by-Step, and PowerLink technologies.

Inclusive Technologies   *www.inclusive.co.uk*

Extensive product line of switch software, alternative keyboards, and other assistive technology tools. Manufactures SwitchIt!

IntelliTools   *www.intellitools.com*

Produces IntelliKeys, an alternative keyboard, as well as other assistive technology tools.

Mayer-Johnson   *www.mayer-johnson.com*

Produces BoardMaker software and other augmentative or alternative communication solutions.

Pro-Ed   *www.proedinc.com*

Manufactures the TouchWindow.

Soft Touch   *www.softtouch.com*

Large selection of switch software and other computer software for students with significant disabilities.

SOURCE: Lisa Barczyk, 2007.

and are convenient when there are multiple switch users in one classroom. Wireless switches use a transmitter and receiver to operate battery-powered and electrical devices, including computers.

▶ Electrical control units act as an interface between an electrical device such as a small appliance, CD player, tape recorder, light, fan, and so on, and a simple switch. The most widely used electrical control unit is the PowerLink by AbleNet. The PowerLink is plugged into a standard electrical outlet. Then the appliance is plugged into the PowerLink and the switch is plugged into the PowerLink, thus making the connection to the appliance. Adjustments on the PowerLink permit the switch user to activate the appliance once, and it will remain on until turned off, or to activate the appliance for a specified amount of time after which it will automatically turn off.

▶ Similar to electrical control units, battery control units act as an interface between a battery-powered toy, game, or device and a simple switch. The most common battery control unit is a switch latch/timer. This device either turns on a device for a specified time period or turns it on or off when the switch is activated. Battery interrupters are inexpensive (approximately $12) and will convert any battery-operated toy or game directly to a switch-controlled device. In that case, the battery control unit is not required.

▶ The following are examples of activities in which environmental controls can be used:

   a. Operating switch-adapted toys—Many switch-adapted toys have an animal theme. With several of them, students using switches can race their animal, measure the distance, and determine a winner. The animals can be further adapted to suit a theme, such as runners in the Olympic Games, astronauts on the moon, fish in the water, and so on.

   b. Playing games—Any battery-operated game can be adapted for switch use with battery interrupters. For card games, a student could use a switch to operate a battery-controlled card shuffler.

   c. Participating in arts and crafts—Students can use a switch-adapted scissors. The paper is held by a classmate while the switch user cuts the paper or other materials for a joint project. The game "Spin Art" can be adapted to use with a switch so that students can create painted designs.

   d. Contributing to a cooking class—Students can make smoothies and milk shakes by using a switch to operate a blender. A specialized pouring switch can be used to measure and pour the ingredients via switch activation. A stand-alone mixer connected to a PowerLink can be used with a switch so that the student can mix ingredients for cakes or cookies.

   e. Making choices—When presented with two or more switch adapted games, students can choose which activity they would prefer. At the computer, the student could decide to listen to music or access a book.

   f. Using a computer—With a switch interface adapter, students can use a switch to activate specialized software games, to scan an onscreen keyboard, or to read an electronic story.

   g. Performing jobs—Using a switch, PowerLink, and paper shredder, students can assist the school office or other teachers with shredding tasks. A popcorn popper, PowerLink, and switch can become a snack cart. Students can make and sell popcorn during special events. A battery-operated coin sorter can be adapted for switch use, and a student could wrap coins from a fund-raising event.

   h. Participating in physical education class—With a switch connected to a CD player or tape recorder, a student can play music for warm-up activities. With a preprogrammed voice output device, a student could lead exercises. Using a switch and PowerLink, a student could operate a fan and cool down classmates after a fun workout.

▶ The student's position while operating a switch is very important. Some will be better at switch activation while supported in a sitting position; others will prefer to stand or lay on their side. The student should use his or her most reliable movement to access the switch. Sometimes, this is not the hand, as might be expected. Some students have better control using their head, elbow, or foot. Trial and error is required and is the best method for determining optimal placement of the switch. Considerable practice opportunities—sometimes hundreds of switch hits per day—are required for students to master effective switch use. For switch use to have meaning, practice should occur during functional activities that are motivating to the student.

Use of Assistive Technology to Hold Things

Students with significant disabilities may have difficulty using their hands to manipulate objects, to hold things, or to let go of things in a precise manner. Assistive technology can provide a solution.

▶ The following are some AT solutions that will enable students to hold things:
   a. Soft tubing, in various diameters, can be placed on handled items such as cooking utensils, eating utensils, crayons and markers, toothbrushes, hairbrushes, and so forth. The larger diameter and softer grip will help the student hold the item in the hand. In addition, Velcro straps can be added to further secure the device.
   b. Using contact paper, sticky-side up, instead of glue will allow students to drop precut shapes or pictures onto the sticky surface where it will adhere with less mess and higher success.

Use of Assistive Technology to See Better

While Braille is the most familiar form of assistive technology for individuals who are blind or visually impaired, most students with significant disabilities will not be able to learn how to use it functionally. Other types of assistive technology may be more appropriate, such as magnification, tactile cues, or voice output.

▶ Magnification can mean the use of magnifying lenses or domes or sheets that are used over printed material. Text on the computer can be enlarged and changed to offsetting, high-contrast colors, such as yellow on black, to aid in visual discrimination.

▶ Tactile cues or different textures can be added to materials to help the student distinguish differences. Tracing simple pictures or shapes with school glue and letting it dry will make a raised outline so that a student could trace over it with his or her finger. Making raised dots of glue in a line will aid students in counting and in learning one-to-one correspondence.

▶ Voice output programs can be used to read text on a computer. There are many options for voice output. Check with your assistive technology consultant or occupational therapist to find out if something like this is available in your school or district.

Use of Assistive Technology to Hear Better

For AT resources in this area, the educational audiologist or teachers of students who are deaf or hearing impaired are the best resources. Because hearing aids and assistive listening devices are so specialized for each individual, it's best to consult with a specialist. As teachers, we know that connecting actions with words and sounds is done throughout the school day and that this helps create an understanding of our world. Consider the following to assist a student with a possible hearing loss to facilitate learning:

▶ Help the student to identify when sounds are used in the routine of the day (when the bell rings, for example) and teach the student an alternative way—using a light flash, for instance—to connect the meaning of the sound to the action. When the bell rings, the student moves to the next class.

▶ Improve the learning environment by reducing background noises. Use a carpet or put tennis balls on the chair legs. Position student close to the front or close to where the sound is located.

▶ Use visual aids—written text, gestures, facial expressions—with auditory information or teaching techniques.

▶ Check with your school to see if the building is equipped with blinking lights for fire or tornado alarms. If not, consider other methods of notifying the student in emergency situations, such as visual aids or signs during drills.

Use of Assistive Technology for Computer Access

A significant amount of resources in the area of assistive technology is devoted to computer access issues. As discussed previously, connecting a switch to the computer will enable a student to play games, scan pictures, or access an electronic book.

▶ The following are other methods of computer access for students with severe disabilities:
  a. Keyboards—Onscreen keyboards are viewed on the computer screen. This is a good option for students who cannot hit the keys of a traditional keyboard but can use a mouse, trackball, or touch screen as an alternative. Onscreen keyboards can also be activated by using visual or auditory scanning with a switch control to select the letter or keystroke. Alternative keyboards are used by students who have difficulty using traditional keyboards. These keyboards can have various layouts, can be designed for one-handed users, and can have larger keys. Some can be programmed. IntelliTools manufactures the IntelliKeys USB alternate keyboard.
  b. Touch screens—Computers can be fitted with a touch screen so that a student can simply point to and touch the computer screen to activate a software program without having to access a keyboard. An example of this type of technology is the TouchWindow by Pro-Ed.

c. Specialized software—Screen readers use voice output technology to read text on the screen; this is very helpful to students who are nonreaders. Switch software is designed to be accessed using a switch. A switch interface must be used for a switch to activate a computer. Some are made to connect one or multiple switches to a single computer, and some are also available in a wireless format. Switch software is used to assist students in learning to use a switch by providing motivating and engaging activities. Products developed by SoftTouch or the SwitchIt! series by Inclusive Technologies are good choices for those new to switch software.

Use of Assistive Technology for Eating or Dressing

Your local medical equipment supply store is the best resource for adaptive equipment used for eating or dressing. Catalogs such as Sammons/Preston/Rolyan and Nasco are also good resources. Consulting with the occupational therapist at your school will also be helpful. The following are some helpful ideas.

► There are specially designed plates with raised edges that make it easier for students to scoop food onto a spoon. Eating utensils come in a wide variety of options. Angled handles help students get food into their mouth without having to turn the spoon or fork; weighted utensils help students with sensory needs or those who have difficulty controlling movement. Rocker knives can be used for cutting food when a student has use of only one hand. Nonskid shelf liners—available at most discount stores—will help hold plates and bowls in place on the table.

► Assistive devices for dressing include buttonhooks that allow students to button clothes using only one hand. Also, using an extra large key ring as a zipper pull works well. It provides a bigger surface for the student to grasp. Elastic shoelaces are very helpful for students who are unable to learn to tie shoes.

Use of Assistive Technology for Access to Recreation and Leisure

Students with significant disabilities who have limited mobility might find it difficult to participate in leisure time activities. There are a variety of assistive technology devices that can provide a solution.

► At home, students can operate warm-water foot massagers with a switch and PowerLink to offer a massage to Mom or Dad or have one themselves.

► Bowling ramps hold a bowling ball so that a student can direct a peer or adult to position the ramp, and then, if able, push the ball so that it rolls down the ramp and onto the bowling lane. Switch-adapted ramps are also available.

► Using cones for playing a game of checkers makes them easier to manipulate; large boards or playing surfaces are also available.

▶ Balls with beepers inside aid students with visual impairments as well as students requiring assistance to focus during a game of catch on the playground or at the park. Beach balls that are very light and of a larger size are great for students with disabilities to use to participate in volleyball or other ball games.

▶ For swimming, flotation vests support the full body and a Head Float by Danmar Products will keep the user's head out of the water and prevent rolling.

Documenting Assistive Technology in the IEP

When assistive technology is used for students with disabilities, the type and amount of AT must be documented in the IEP. There are several ways to do this. For example, keeping a dated log of the devices and services that have been tried will help guide future decisions about the amount or type of assistive technology that the student requires. This log should be reviewed on a regular basis and especially when the student moves to a different classroom or learning environment. Be sure to consult your supervisor or principal to determine the specific documentation policies of your school district.

▶ If a student currently uses AT, the type or amount should be included in the statement of present levels of academic achievement and functional performance. For example, if the student is using a single-switch voice output device for communication, a statement such as "student activates a single-switch voice output device positioned near his right hand to greet teachers and peers 8–10 times per day" should be included in the IEP.

▶ AT can also be included in the goals and objectives of the IEP. For example, "With a built-up handle spoon, student will scoop 5 spoons of pudding," or "With a simple switch mounted on the left side of the headrest and connected to an electrical control, student will operate office equipment such as a paper shredder or electric stapler to assist with classroom jobs."

▶ Assistive technology can also be a related service, such as when someone is required to set up or program the equipment a student may be using. AT as a related service occurs most often for students who use AT for communication.

▶ Identifying specific devices or equipment should only be done in the IEP if that particular device has features that are so unique, no other similar device could be used. For example, it is not necessary to give a name brand of a particular switch if any simple switch will meet the student's need. This allows for flexibility on the part of the school to use a variety of options as long as the type of equipment is available.

▶ The WATI Assessment Form, developed by the Wisconsin Assistive Technology Initiative, is a resource to assist IEP teams in considering the need for assistive technology. A sample form is included at the end of this chapter—see Figure 6.2— and is also available online at the WATI website, www.wati.org.

Figure 6.2 WATI Assistive Technology Consideration Guide

WATI Assessment Forms

WISCONSIN ASSISTIVE
WATI
TECHNOLOGY INITIATIVE

WATI Assistive Technology Consideration Guide

Student's Name _____ School _____

1. What task is it that we want this student to do, that s/he is unable to do at a level that reflects his/her skills/abilities (writing, reading, communicating, seeing, hearing)? Document by checking each relevant task below. Please leave blank any tasks that are not relevant to the student's IEP.

2. Is the student currently able to complete tasks with special strategies or accommodations? If yes, describe in Column A for each checked task.

3. Is there available assistive technology (either devices, tools, hardware, of software) that could be used to address this task? (If none are known, review WATI's AT Checklist.) If any assistive technology tools are currently being used (or were tried in the past), describe in Column B.

4. Would the use of assistive technology help the student perform this skill more easily or efficiently, in the least restrictive environment, or perform successfully with less personal assistance? If yes, complete Column C.

Task	A. If currently completes task with special strategies/accommodations, describe.	B. If currently completes task with assistive technology tools, describe.	C. Describe new or additional assistive technology to be tried.
☐ Motor Aspects of Writing			
☐ Computer Access			
☐ Composing Written Material			
☐ Communication			
☐ Reading			
☐ Learning/Studying			

Task	A. If currently completes task with special strategies/accommodations, describe.	B. If currently completes task with assistive technology tools, describe.	C. Describe new or additional assistive technology to be tried.
☐ Math			
☐ Recreation and Leisure			
☐ Activities of Daily Living (ADLs)			
☐ Mobility			
☐ Environmental Control			
☐ Positioning and Seating			
☐ Vision			
☐ Hearing			

5. Are there assistive technology services (more specific evaluation of need for assistive technology, adapting or modifying the assistive technology, technical assistance on its operation or use, or training of student, staff, or family) that this student needs? If yes, describe what will be provided, the initiation and duration.

_____

Persons Present: _____   Date: _____

7

Understanding Behavior

S tudents with significant disabilities may have extreme behaviors that need to be anticipated and managed within a variety of settings. These behaviors can range from making loud noises or screaming to self-abusive behaviors like head banging. The most important things to consider are the communication intent of these behaviors; the demands of the physical environment; and sometimes, the relationship to the specific disability or syndrome. As the teacher, you must consider the support or interventions in each setting that are needed to provide a successful learning experience for all students. The suggestions in this chapter encourage positive interventions for significant behaviors to enable teaching and learning to occur.

Chapter Outline

- Communication
- Determining Cause and Supporting the Student
- Developing a Support Plan for Difficult Behaviors in Different Settings
- Shaping Behavior and Rewards

Communication

It is important to know that specific behaviors and the interpretation of these behaviors may be different for teachers, parents, and students. As the teacher, you must try to interpret the student's communication intent with specific behaviors. For students with significant disabilities, it is safe to assume that all behaviors are methods of communication for them. Consider the following points that can help prevent misinterpretation of behaviors.

▶ Use explicit directions. For example, saying "Let's get ready to go out for recess" might not elicit a response from a student with a significant disability. He or she is not being stubborn, noncompliant, or difficult. Rather, the student may not understand the directions because of the multiple concepts of get ready, go out, and recess. State explicit directions such as "Please put your coat on," and provide visual and physical cues or gestures if needed.

▶ Consider contextual cues or situations and the demands of different environments, and remember that behaviors may occur in certain situations and not others. For example, the presence or absence of certain people, a specific time of day, a specific environment, a certain noise or lighting of a room, or other factors can contribute to a behavior occurring. Students with significant disabilities may be exhibiting behavior to communicate a need or concern. The student may be communicating that he or she is frustrated, hurt, hungry, excited, sad, and so on. Try to determine which variable contributes to the behavior, and prepare the student by telling or showing him or her in advance what can be expected or what will happen, or by offering a preferred activity in that particular situation. Much of this process is trial and error. A student showing signs of discomfort might require more frequent position changes, but a student who screams when seeing his or her standing frame might require encouragement to stand for a short while and work through the behavior.

▶ Consider various methods of communication for students who do not use traditional modes, such as pictures or voice output technology. Allow enough time for these methods of communication to be used throughout lessons and activities. Provide the student opportunities for ongoing practice with appropriate communication throughout the day by incorporating the communication method into as many activities as possible.

▶ Always remember to consult with family members and others who are significant to the student. First, determine if they see the same behavior, and if so, when it occurs. Next, brainstorm to clarify the communication intent or the need of the student. Then, develop consistent strategies to cope with or minimize the behavior. Also, be conscious of the student's cultural background. Certain behaviors might be acceptable in the home environment and not in school settings.

Determining Cause and Supporting the Student

The context of when and where behaviors occur can play a key role in determining what your student needs. As the teacher, your goal should be to understand where and when the behavior occurs, and plan for the student's need

with strategies to help him or her cope in specific situations. Consider the following points to determine the cause and some positive strategies to support the student.

▶ First, get to know the student as a human being; become familiar with the situations that have influenced his or her life thus far. It is also important to define the specific behavior(s) that seems to be a challenge for the student with a significant disability or for the other students around him or her.

▶ Realize that many times behaviors occur because students are missing something in their life. Consider the person's quality of life and quality of involvement during the school day. David Pitonyak (2007) states that people with difficult behaviors are often missing the following:
   a. Meaningful relationships
   b. A sense of safety and well-being
   c. A sense of their own power
   d. Things to look forward to
   e. A sense of value and self-worth
   f. Relevant skills and knowledge
   g. Supporters who are themselves supported

▶ Gather detailed data to identify specific times, days, or situations when the identified behavior is occurring. Figure 7.1 can be used to collect data. In the A (antecedent) column, document the time, day, and what takes place right before the behavior occurs. Next, list the defined behavior(s) that occur. Finally, state the consequence (negative or positive) that occurs after the behavior. For example, the student was told to stop biting his or her hand or the student was given time in the quiet area of the class and allowed the choice of looking at a magazine or listening to music. See Figure 7.2 for a sample of a completed behavior log.

▶ Ask questions and share information about the behavior(s) with family or other key persons in the student's life. Find out if there are similar times, contexts, or situations in which the behavior occurs.

▶ Consider the following positive ways to support a student and behaviors outlined by Paula Kluth (2003):
   a. If possible, ask the student about the behavior, or ask the student to describe how he or she is feeling to gain some insight as to why the behaviors may be occurring.
   b. Make the most of school and community supports. Sometimes other peers or school staff can offer comfort or understanding that you as the teacher might not be able to give the student.
   c. Make connections, and form a relationship with the student. The best way to understand specific behaviors is to seek ways to connect with the student, and build a strong relationship. This is sometimes very difficult, but it is critical when students do not have a reliable way to communicate. Build relationships by greeting students as they enter the room, make a list of caring words to describe students, and be a good listener.
   d. Be gentle and understanding in a crisis. Consider your body language as well as the tone and loudness of your voice. Do not use punitive or demeaning statements. Try to redirect the student toward something positive or comforting.

e. Consider perception and language. Many times specific behaviors can cause others to perceive a student in a negative way. Try to explain the meaning of the behavior to them. Also, avoid using the "us and them" language (Shevin, 1987). For example, "They self-stim; we fidget." Instead, discuss things the student can do and the positive attributes they can offer to the group.

f. Teach new skills, and be willing to adapt. For example, if a student has a difficult time getting involved at recess, teach him or her how to use the slide, or teach the student a new game. Adapt an activity that proves difficult and frustrating for the student. For example, if a student is afraid of elevators, show the student how to use the steps or an escalator. If a student cannot write his or her name on the top of a paper, provide a stamp or preprinted label.

g. Take care of yourself, and allow time for relaxation. Take a deep breath, and think about the situation. As teachers, we will not always have the answers, and some days will be tougher than others.

Developing a Support Plan for Difficult Behaviors in Different Settings

Keep in mind that you will not be able to eliminate all negative behaviors completely. However, some serious behaviors such as biting or pinching others and spitting or hitting must be eliminated in order for the student to have successful learning opportunities with his or her peers. Other less serious behaviors such as talking out of turn or making loud noises can be modified by teaching the student replacement behaviors. Develop a plan to follow within different instructional settings to address these behaviors when they occur. Students should not lose privileges or be removed from environments to eliminate behaviors, as these are only short-term solutions. Consider the following strategies.

▶ Students should not be escorted out of a room or an environment every time a negative behavior occurs. Provide the student with consistent, sequential responses that include verbal, visual, and physical prompts and redirection. When teaching replacement behaviors, be consistent in all environments. For example, if the student is being taught to bite on a washcloth instead of on him- or herself or others, have washcloths readily available in all environments.

▶ Understand when and why behaviors occur. Develop a plan of support and a backup plan for the instructional environments. Discuss this plan with all support staff so that everyone is consistent.

▶ With the support staff, discuss the signs that could indicate a student is becoming agitated. Outline specific strategies that should be used at this point to eliminate the behavior or to help the student cope with the situation. Interventions should occur before the behavior escalates. For less serious behaviors, do not always make a student's success depend on total compliance.

▶ Some days are better than others for all of us. There might be certain times or days when you will need to alter expectations of your students in order for them to be successful.

▶ David Pitonyak (n.d.) offers forms that can be used to develop a support plan. The direct link to this website resource is http://dimagine.com/Support%20Plan%20Forms.pdf.

Figure 7.1 Behavior Log

Student: _____

Define Behavior(s): _____

_____

_____

Date/ Day/Time	What happens before the behavior? (Antecedent)	Behavior	What happens after behavior occurs? (Consequence)

Figure 7.2   Sample Behavior Log

Student: Robert

Define Behavior(s):   Spitting

                      Loud vocalizations and pulling own hair

Date/ Day/Time	What happens before the behavior? (Antecedent)	Behavior	What happens after behavior occurs? (Consequence)
10/7/07 Monday 12:40 PM	Teacher told students they would need to get up and go to gym	Loud vocalization; began pulling own hair	Teacher walked near Robert, gave verbal cue, "We are going to gym—please put hands at your side."
10/7/07 12:45 PM	Walking in hall to gym	Spit at another student	Other students became verbal and loud, told Robert to stop. Teacher walked near Robert, but gave him no eye contact or verbal cue.
10/10/07 Thursday 11:00 AM	Teacher said, "Time to go to lunch" and turned off the classroom lights.	Loud vocalization; began pulling hair	Teacher asked Robert to stand and go to lunch, and to please put his hands at his side.

SOURCE: Michele Flasch Ziegler, 2007.

Shaping Behavior and Rewards

Behavior cannot always be controlled by the student or by the teacher. When dealing with behavior, we need to consider the depth of social situations, including all the factors that may contribute to the circumstances such as the disability, the environment, the demands, social relationships, and so on. Some elements of behaviorism and theories such as B. F. Skinner's operant conditioning might be useful and should be considered but should not be used in isolation. Here are some additional suggestions for handling behavior issues.

▶   Develop consistent routines and structures within your school day and week to help students learn what to expect.

▶   Be a sensitive teacher and don't react negatively to behaviors. Instead, develop positive supports and teaching strategies.

▶ In general, using rewards and reinforcement to change students' behavior long term will not be successful and might prove frustrating for you as the teacher. There are many variables in the day-to-day life of each student that can cause his or her motivation to change across settings, people involved, and so forth. Reinforcements might not always work. Help your students, and teach them to monitor their own behavior and to learn from the natural consequences of their actions.

▶ Try not to use punishment to change behavior. It doesn't provide a positive way for students to learn what is expected of them. Instead, model the appropriate behavior or an alternative behavior that you want the student to use; offer praise when the student complies with one of these.

▶ Remember that all the data collection and behavioral techniques in the world are not as important as helping your students to achieve a good quality of life.

8

Working With Related Service Providers and Other Support Staff

S tudents with multiple and significant disabilities often receive services at school from specialists such as therapists and other support personnel. In the IEP, this support is called related services. Teachers and therapists must work together as a team so that the student receives a coordinated educational program focused on the integrated goals of the student's IEP.

Chapter Outline

- Defining Related Services

- Models of Service Delivery

- Teacher Tips for Working With Related Service Providers

- Finding Time for Collaboration

- Role of the Occupational Therapist

- ■ Role of the Physical Therapist
- ■ Role of the Speech and Language Pathologist
- ■ Working With Other Support Personnel

Defining Related Services

Related services are the specific supports designed to help a student benefit from his or her special education program. They cover a broad spectrum of assistance that can include therapeutic and health-related interventions.

▶ The IEP team must consider if students requiring special education services also require related services. IDEIA 2004 defines related services as "transportation, and such developmental, corrective, and other supportive services (including speech-language pathology and audiology services, interpreting services, psychological services, physical and occupational therapy, recreation, including therapeutic recreation, social work services, school nurse services) designed to enable a child with a disability to receive a free appropriate public education as described in the individualized education program of the child, counseling services, including rehabilitation counseling, orientation and mobility services, and medical services (except that such medical services shall be for diagnostic and evaluation purposes only) as may be required to assist a child with a disability to benefit from special education, and includes the early identification and assessment of disabling conditions in children." The one exception is that the term "does not include a medical device that is surgically implanted or the replacement of such device."

▶ The IEP team determines the type, frequency, and amount of related services that the student will require to benefit from his or her special education program. Generally, the therapist or other specialist will make a recommendation to the team regarding the frequency and amount of services. This recommendation is based in part on an evaluation of the student's functional performance at school in relation to the service being considered. To make a determination of the need for related services, the team further considers the student's current IEP goals, history of progress toward meeting goals, and overall functional performance at school.

▶ Students with significant disabilities often receive occupational therapy, physical therapy, or speech and language therapy. Additional services such as support for mobility or vision or hearing impairments might also be provided. It can be a challenge to coordinate schedules so that the student is able to receive the required services and the professionals involved can find the necessary time to collaborate. See further discussion under Finding Time for Collaboration in this chapter.

Models of Service Delivery

The IEP team makes a determination of how and where the student will receive the identified related services. For most students, this is a combination of individual or small-group time with the specialist (resource model) and time within the student's learning environment (integrated services).

▶ The resource method is most consistent with how services are delivered to students in a medical model. Most specialists have spent at least some portion of their careers working in medical facilities or clinics where the student arrives, receives services, and leaves. The specialist works with the student 1:1 or in small groups, and the focus of the intervention is on addressing impairments such as decreased strength, limited movement, or lack of vocalizations. Any functional skills that can be addressed are specific to the clinical environment. When the first federal special education laws went into effect in 1975, therapists arrived in schools bringing with them the medical model of service delivery that became know in schools as the "pull-out"—now referred to as resource—model. In turn, teachers also believed that special education students had to go somewhere else to learn specific skills with a therapist.

▶ With a resource model of service delivery at school, students are removed from the classroom or other learning environment, and as a result they miss whatever instruction occurs while they are away. In this separate setting, specialists tend to focus only on the student's needs relating to the service being provided. Occupational therapists (OTs) will work on fine motor or self-help skills; physical therapists (PTs) will provide exercises or games aimed toward movement and mobility; and speech therapists will focus on sound production or use of communication aids. All of these activities are valid and appropriate. The issue is whether or not the student achieves as much benefit from the service when it is provided away from the classroom setting and disconnected from the student's typical learning environment as the student would if he or she remained in the classroom.

▶ Recent trends in special education have led to a preference for the integrated services model, and there are many advantages to providing related services in the setting in which the student must learn to function, especially when the student has significant and multiple disabilities. Consider what model is in use in your school. If the integrated model is not being used, you might want to consider opening a dialogue with your administration or other involved professionals to discuss the advantages of using this model if it would best fit the needs of your students.

▶ The following are benefits to choosing an integrated services model:
   a. The student has a consistent learning environment and routine and does not miss part of the educational day.
   b. The specialist is able to identify any environmental barriers to learning and can problem solve with the team on how to eliminate these barriers. For example, a therapist might suggest the use of vertical shelving so that a student can access and choose similar materials when in a wheelchair or when positioned on the floor. Vertical shelving means that common materials such as books, puzzles, manipulatives, art supplies, and so on are arranged top to bottom on three or four shelves—such as on a bookcase— instead of the same type of item using the length of one whole shelf.
   c. The student can practice generalizing skills with different people within a common environment. Opportunities to practice communication skills with a variety of people lead to increased social awareness and interaction.
   d. Specialists gain direct knowledge of what is expected of the student in a specific environment. It is important for therapists to know what tasks the student is required to complete so that interventions can be aimed at achieving the skills with the most functional benefit.

e. The specialist is in the best position to assist the student in completing the required tasks. Classroom activities become therapeutic activities when the therapist is actively involved with the student.

f. The specialist can choose an environment where the service is of most benefit to the student. It is not uncommon to find the OT in the lunchroom, the PT in the gym, or the speech therapist in music class.

g. The teacher and classroom support staff are present and can observe how the specialist works with the student to achieve desired outcomes. Therapists can suggest and demonstrate related activities for the student to practice when the therapist is not there.

h. Progress monitoring is easier to achieve and is functionally based.

i. The effects of the service intervention are apparent in a functional setting. In the general education setting, there is an incidental benefit to all students as well.

j. The ability to collaborate as a team by sharing expertise and ideas on behalf of a student with significant disabilities also provides incidental benefit to all students and staff in the general education classroom.

▶ The specific needs of the student in terms of functional goals and necessary supports should be the determining factors of the location and model of related services delivery.

Teacher Tips for Working With Related Service Providers

Establishing positive working relationships with related service providers is a key component to successful IEP teams and to positive student outcomes. The following suggestions are offered as strategies to help teachers coordinate the various services a student may receive.

▶ Check the student's IEPs to find out which related services are required as well as the amount and frequency of the services. Then make sure these requirements are being met by the service providers. Incorporate the services into the IEP-at-a-glance (see Figure 1.2). This will provide all involved professionals with the opportunity to know the full scope of services the student receives.

▶ Talk to the service providers, and discuss collaboration on initial and ongoing training of support staff. If something related to the care of a student is unfamiliar to you, write it down on a training-needs list and show the list to the providers when they come into your classroom. (See Figure 8.1 for a sample training-needs list.)

▶ Discuss scheduling, and notify providers of any upcoming IEP team meetings, giving enough notice for them to rearrange their schedules so they can participate in the meetings. Remember that therapists may serve more than one school building, especially in large urban school districts.

▶ Ask for the provider's contact information—telephone, voicemail, cell phone, pager, e-mail address, and so on. Keep a list of the contact information for all the providers that serve students on your caseload so you can readily reach them when needed.

▶ Give the related service providers a general schedule that the student will be following so the student can be located to receive services. Inform providers of schedule changes such as field trips or special school activities in which the student will be involved at a time that would interfere with the scheduled therapy service (see Figure 8.2).

Figure 8.1 Sample Training-Needs List

Training Topic/Issue	Related Service Provider Requested (circle)		Specific Student (indicate name/s of student/s)	Staff Members to Include	Date Requested	Date Completed
Wheelchair Transfers and Lifting Techniques	OT PT SLP	Hearing Vision Other:				
Positioning Equipment (circle):	OT PT SLP	Hearing Vision Other:				
Stander Floor sitter Side-lyer	OT PT SLP	Hearing Vision Other:				
Assistive Technology: Communication and/or Other devices	OT PT SLP	Hearing Vision Other:				
Adapted Materials: Classroom and/or Vocational	OT PT SLP	Hearing Vision Other:				

SOURCE: Lisa Barczyk, 2007.

Figure 8.2 Alternate Activity Communication Form

TO: _____
      (related services provider)

_____ will be gone from school on a **field trip** during
(student name)

therapy time on _____.
         (date)

_____will not be available during
(student name)

therapy time on_____due to **testing, in-school assembly, other**.
        (date)   (circle one)

Please return this form with an alternate time for the therapy session:

_____
(date and time)

SOURCE: Lisa Barczyk, 2007.

Finding Time for Collaboration

Teachers and related service providers struggle with finding time to communicate or to get together for consultation and planning. It is necessary to be creative and also to recognize that time might have to be scheduled outside of the school day. The key is planning. If meetings are scheduled regularly and the agenda is followed, the actual time required will not be as overwhelming. Here are some suggestions for creating collaborative time.

▶ Use written communication as much as possible for specific questions and answers that do not require a face-to-face meeting. Three good ways of doing this are as follows:
   a. Share e-mail addresses with providers.
   b. Keep a notebook or binder in the classroom that can be used for questions and answers exchanged between you and the specialists.
   c. If the service providers have mailboxes, use them as a way to communicate.

▶ Schedule a regular meeting time such as the second Tuesday of the month after school or the first Thursday before school. This allows everyone to put the permanent meeting date and time on their calendar, making it much easier for them to remember every month.

▶ Have lunch together in the teacher's lounge once every month. Or if this isn't the best location for a private conversation, use your classroom or one of the therapy rooms if possible.

▶ Meet on the playground during recess occasionally. Even if you regularly hold your meeting someplace else, arrange to gather on the playground once in a while to observe student interaction in an unstructured setting.

▶ Partner with another teacher, and take turns covering the classroom while giving the other teacher time to meet with the specialists. Remember that good communication leads to quality collaboration that produces positive outcomes for students.

Role of the Occupational Therapist

For students with significant disabilities, occupational therapists focus on the routines of daily life in the student's learning environments, generally with a heavy focus on assistive technology. (See Chapter 6 for additional AT information.)

▶ The OT can help the student access and use classroom materials such as books, desk supplies, toys, and games as well as provide assistance in other important areas. The following are some of the ways the OT can help:
   a. When students cannot use their hands effectively to manipulate objects in the environment, the OT might try exercises or specially designed splints to help the student keep his or her hand open or more easily close the hand around an object. Ask the OT about a wearing schedule for hand splints. Most students will not need to wear splints all day, and it is important to follow the instructions for when and where the splints should be used.

    b. Some students will require alternative methods to access and use classroom materials. The OT can develop alternative methods for the student to fully or partially participate through adaptations such as designing specialized hand grips, placing knobs on puzzle pieces, or adapting books and games.

    c. The OT can also work with the student and the teacher to develop the best routine for managing self-care. It is important for the student to practice the agreed-upon routine at the appropriate times of the day. For example, the OT may suggest adaptive eating supplies such as specially designed utensils, dishes, or bowls and can teach strategies for facilitating self-feeding that can be implemented at lunch time.

    d. The OT can assist with strategies for sensory processing, such as responses to touch, sound, sight, and movement. While multisensory environments are generally good for learning, some settings can be overwhelming for students who do not process sensory information in the same way as their peers do. The OT can suggest many strategies to help students cope with over- or underreactive sensory systems. For example, providing a verbal warning before using hand-over-hand assistance can give the student an opportunity to prepare for being touched.

    e. The OT can assist with job skills training. Students with significant disabilities will require assistance with setting up work so that the materials are within their reach and visual field. OTs can also create adaptations to the job such as using cardboard tubes to hold bags open so they can be filled. Students may require assistance with staying on task until the job is complete. OTs often use visual strategies to sequence the steps of the job, or timers to help the student know when to stop or to indicate the time to take a break from the work.

▶ OTs are skilled in task analysis and can break down a complex task into manageable pieces. Provide a list of classroom jobs routinely given to students, and the OT will be able to adapt at least a few of them so a student with significant disabilities can share the job responsibilities in the class. For example, one student responsibility might be to take attendance each day. The OT might suggest the use of a step-by-step communicator that can be programmed with each student's name, and the student completing the job would activate the switch to call the roll.

▶ Be sure you get to know the OT in your building as soon as possible. Most likely this person will be important in the school life of your students and will be able to provide you with good ideas and strategies that will enhance your teaching.

Role of the Physical Therapist

For students with significant disabilities, physical therapists focus on positioning, movement, travel, and access. By evaluating the student's strength, endurance, balance, and movement patterns, PTs are able to recommend activities and positions that will enhance the student's ability to learn and to participate in the classroom routines.

▶ Students who have limited independent movement often cannot reposition themselves throughout the day. Think of how many times you shift on your chair, get up and sit down, stretch, and just generally move around during your day. Repositioning is necessary to keep our circulation operating smoothly and to prevent soreness. Physical therapists will train teachers and classroom support staff on the proper methods for assisting students in repositioning throughout the school day. The therapists also provide training on safe lifting techniques to classroom teachers and classroom support staff members. For some students, mechanical lifts may be required for the safety of the student and the staff. Remember to locate positioning or lifting equipment in the environment in which the student will be using it. Keep a box of extra pillows, towels, cushions, and safety straps handy in case the student requires a quick repositioning.

▶ For students with significant physical disabilities, establishing even one reliable movement will provide opportunities for communication and require access to materials. Through evaluation and intervention, a physical therapist can assist a student in establishing reliable movements of the eyes, head, arm, hand, or leg so that the student can learn how to operate a communication device or activate a switch to gain partial or active participation in functional activities. Observe the student, and record which movements you see most often. Then share this information with the PT as you work together to assist the student in developing reliable movements.

▶ Students with significant disabilities who are wheelchair users generally have wheelchairs that are pushed by others (manual wheelchairs) for travel. Physical therapists work with students, families, and equipment vendors to ensure that the appropriate wheelchair has been selected and that the seating system meets the needs of the student. Seating systems and wheelchairs are reevaluated on an ongoing basis to ensure proper fit, comfort, and safety. Keep a clipboard with a list of wheelchair issues such as loose straps, brakes that aren't working properly, seatbelts that do not fit, missing parts, and so forth so that the PT can be made aware of them and contact equipment vendors for the needed repairs.

▶ The physical therapist will evaluate any environmental barriers that might be present in the school such as those regarding access to the bathrooms, exiting the building in an emergency, negotiating the uneven surfaces of a playground, maneuvering efficiently in the lunchroom, and so on. Ask the PT to do a walk-through of the hallways, classrooms, bathrooms, lunchroom, recess area, bus loading area, and so on, to determine in advance if any accommodations will be necessary for student access.

Role of the Speech and Language Pathologist

If all my possessions were taken from me with one exception, I would choose to keep the power of communication, for by it I would soon regain all the rest.

Daniel Webster

Through communication, individuals express what they need or want and interact socially with others. They also receive information that helps them learn

and communicate reciprocally. The speech and language pathologist (SLP) works with the classroom staff to determine how the student with significant disabilities is choosing to communicate, how the student receives information, how others understand the communication, and how communication can be improved over time. The SLP can assist you with understanding or implementing any of the following information or ideas:

▶ It is important to recognize how the student is choosing to communicate. Students with significant disabilities will likely communicate nonverbally. Some examples of nonverbal communication are

    a. Eye gaze—The student will look at someone nearby, at an object, or toward a location during a time of communication.

    b. Facial expression—The student uses any part of the face to communicate such as smiling, grimacing, or raising eyebrows.

    c. Vocalization—The student uses unintelligible vocal sounds; sometimes the same sound may have more than one intention.

    d. Pointing—The student uses any body part—hand, finger, leg, foot—to extend toward a person, object, or location in a communicating way.

    e. Gestures—The student uses conventional signals that are widely understood such as shaking head back and forth for no, nodding head up and down for yes, hand or arm up for stop, and so forth.

    f. Objects—The student uses actual objects to represent an activity, need, or want. Some examples would be using a CD to ask for music, a ball for play or for recess, a spoon for eating or for lunch, or a book for reading.

    g. Pictures—The student uses actual pictures or photographs of objects, activities, or people to communicate.

    h. Picture representations—The student uses drawings or symbols of objects, activities, or people to communicate.

▶ It is also necessary to know how the student receives information. Most teachers in general and special education use verbal presentation of material as the primary method of education in the classroom. For students with significant disabilities, too much verbal information will not be processed in a meaningful way for them. Visual or tactile information must also be used to ensure the student will understand. Suggestions for adding this kind of information for instruction in general education are as follows:

    a. Make props for a story that students can hold and manipulate while the book is read.

    b. Create a communication board with pictures or symbols from the story that the student can match with pictures in the book or can use to answer questions about the story.

    c. Label objects in the environment with words or pictures.

    d. Invest in a digital camera, or ask for one at your school. Take pictures to use for visual schedules, or use photos from the classroom to make personalized books. (See Chapter 2, Organizing the Students and Their Learning Environment.)

    e. Ask general education teachers to use more exaggerated gestures, such as holding up hands to ask where or emphatically shaking their head for no.

    f. Demonstrate what the student should do—resist the temptation to continue repeating verbal directions.

g. Be sure you and your assistants are in close proximity to the student for effective communication.

▶ Interpreting nonverbal communication is very challenging. The Provincial Integration Support Program in Canada suggests the use of a personal dictionary as a reference guide for those communicating with nonverbal students. (Their website is www.pisp.ca; see Figure 8.3.) The creation of a student's personal dictionary requires input from individuals who know the student best and from those who have well-developed observational skills.

▶ Helping students to improve their communication skills is an important goal. The SLP helps the team determine how to assist the student with developing a communication system. For communication to be effective, it must be consistent. The student will need to practice communication skills in all environments all of the time. Some suggestions for practicing communication skills are as follows:

a. Whenever feasible, offer choices. If a student is using actual objects, pictures, or picture representations, have a large supply of those items on hand. Choice making should happen throughout the day, and the student can use any method of communication described above to make the choices. Remember that the student should always be given a choice as the outcome of the communication. For example,

1. "Which book would you like to read?" Offer a choice of two with one being a known favorite. Increase the choices as the student becomes more proficient.

2. "Do you want applesauce or a drink?" Let the student make the selection. If the student refuses the selection, offer again, but say, "Sam, you chose this. Do you want to make a different choice?"

b. Practice social interactions. Some students will need to develop consistency in paying attention to another person such as a peer partner in class. This is the beginning of learning to take turns and understanding the flow of conversation. Offering a greeting or saying good-bye is another natural interaction that students with significant disabilities can practice many times per day. The following are some examples of how to practice social interaction with your students.

1. Pair the student with a peer. Then ask the peer to read a book aloud, stopping when the student is not attending to him or her. The reader then gets the student's attention and continues reading. Demonstration may be necessary depending on the age of the students.

2. Talk with selected staff members throughout the school. Ask them to greet the student, wait patiently for a response in whatever method the student is using to communicate, then acknowledge the student's response, and continue on. Students with significant disabilities will likely have delays in auditory processing time, so it's necessary to wait for a response, and resist the urge to repeat the interaction. Saying it again means that the student has to start processing all over again, and frustration will result.

▶ Remember that behavior is also communication. Students who are nonverbal use whatever methods available to them to communicate with the world. Sometimes, their communication is a behavior that is unacceptable such as hitting, biting, or spitting. Discovering the meaning behind the adverse behaviors is essential to establishing more efficient and acceptable methods of communication. (See Chapter 7, Understanding Behavior.)

Working With Other Support Personnel

Additional support staff may be a part of the students' educational team such as teachers of students who are blind or visually impaired, teachers of students who are deaf or hearing impaired, art therapists, music therapists, and others. These support people may be full- or part-time at your school, or they might be contract employees. If you have students who have visual or hearing impairments but have no resource people at your school who can help you, speak to your school administrator or your special education administrator.

▶ Some students with significant disabilities will have visual impairments. When the problem is diagnosed as a cortical vision impairment, it means that the student's visual skills are inconsistent—sometimes they are able to see, and sometimes they cannot; but color vision is not typically affected. This is due to malfunction of the connection between the brain and the eye. Teachers of the blind or visually impaired will be able to offer suggestions about how materials should be presented to the student, providing tactile or auditory choices due to the student's unreliable vision. Equipment such as enlarged printed materials or light boxes may be used. The following are some suggestions that might be helpful for students with vision impairments.

　　a. Make sure students are positioned appropriately to receive information presented visually. Some students will see better with peripheral vision and require materials to be placed to the side rather than directly in front of them. Most students will benefit from materials placed close to them.

　　b. Reduce visual clutter by presenting materials one at a time or using high contrasts such as white on black or yellow on black.

　　c. Consider sunglasses or hats/visors if the student appears unusually sensitive to sunlight or bright light in the classroom or school.

▶ Students with a diagnosed visual impairment may also receive services from orientation and mobility specialists. These professionals teach the student how to navigate in a variety of environments. For students with significant disabilities, the specialist will work closely with the physical therapist to determine the student's most effective method of mobility.

▶ Using conventional sign language is often ineffective with students who have significant disabilities. Teachers of those who are deaf or hearing impaired may suggest developing gestures that are meaningful to the activity and adapting learning materials to have more of a visual or tactile focus. They are also able to provide training to other students and staff about how to communicate with someone who is deaf or hearing impaired. The following are some suggestions that might be helpful for students with hearing impairments:

　　a. Consult with the school's audiologist if assistive listening devices are being considered. If there is no audiologist on staff, ask your building

Figure 8.3 Personal Dictionary

Personal Dictionary (Communicative Intent Log) Sample

Student: _____

Birthdate: _____ Date: _____

Behaviors Observed "This is what I do"	Intent/What It Means This is what I am trying to tell you.	How To Respond What you can say and/or do 1. Identify behavior 2. Interpret behavior 3. Respond
1. Looking away, turns head away	Not interested in activity	• "J," you're looking away. • You're telling me you don't like _____. • Let's see if there is something else you like better. (Offer "J" a choice of a different activity.)
2. Head down, hands sometimes in mouth, eyes closed	a) Tired, sleepy b) Bored, not interested in activity	a) "J," you're closing your eyes and putting your head down. • You must be tired. • Give "J" 15–20 min. rest before starting another activity. b) "J," you're closing your eyes and putting your head down. • I think you must be bored with _____. • Two more min. & we'll switch to something else. (Attempt to challenge "J" to continue with activity for a bit longer before switching to next activity or offering a choice.)
3. Finger or thumb in mouth, low pitched hum	Unhappy, wants out of wheelchair and to be left alone	a) "J," your finger is in your mouth & you are humming. • You want out of your chair and some time on your own. • Take "J" out of wheelchair & put "J" on floor. Try not to disturb him for 15–20 min. b) "J," your finger is in your mouth & you are humming. • "J," you're telling me you want out of your chair but we need to finish this & then we'll get out onto the floor. c) "J," your finger is in your mouth & you are humming. • You want out of your chair & some time on your own. • We were just on the floor; now it is time to work in your chair. When we finish, then we'll take another break.
4. Loud, low pitched vocalization (whining), rocking in chair, agitated facial expression	I'm hungry and I want to eat now.	• "J," I can tell by your face and voice that you're not happy. • Get "J" something to eat ASAP.
5. Sticking out tongue while drinking	I don't want any more to drink.	• "J," you're sticking your tongue out. • I think you're saying you don't want any more to drink. • Stop giving "J" a drink. If he hasn't had much to drink, offer more in about 30–45 min. or at the end of the meal.

PROVINCIAL INTEGRATION SUPPORT PROGRAM SCHOOL DISTRICT 61

SOURCE: Reprinted with permission from the Provincial Integration Support Program, B.C. Ministry of Education (www.pisp.ca).

administrator or your special education administrator how this service can be provided.

b. Pair verbal instruction with visual or tactile cues.

c. Try to avoid noisy environments during instruction time.

▶ Note that for students who are deaf-blind, very specialized approaches are required to find the best strategies for teaching and learning. Teachers of the blind and deaf will be most effective. Again, if no one with this expertise is on your school staff, ask your building administrator or your special education administrator how this service can be provided.

▶ Specially designed or adapted physical education is provided to students with significant and multiple disabilities. This means that the student is unable to participate in the general physical education curriculum and must have skills and activities modified for learning. Licensure requirements for the delivery of adaptive physical education vary among the states. Check with your school's physical education teacher to determine who will be providing this service to your students.

▶ The IEP team might determine that a student with significant and multiple disabilities requires art or music therapy to benefit from his or her special education program. Check with your special education administrative team to find out if these kinds of therapists are employed by your school district or if services are contracted or provided in other ways.

Not all students will receive all of the services described in this chapter. A related service is provided when it is required for the student to benefit from special education. The IEP team determines the type, amount, frequency, and location of each service and bases its decision on the student's educational plan. The decision to include or not include a particular related service is made after the student's goals and objectives have been determined. It is appropriate for the type, amount, and frequency of services to change over time as the student's priority needs also change.

9

Communication With Parents and Guardians

Developing constructive relationships with parents and guardians is very important to the success of your students. Ongoing communication, using various methods and strategies, will help coordinate expectations both at school and at home. This chapter will focus on developing positive connections with families.

Chapter Outline

- Developing a Positive Relationship With Parents or Guardians
- Coordinating School and Home Expectations
- Ongoing Communication Strategies
- IEP Team Meetings
- Parent–Teacher Conferences

Developing a Positive Relationship
With Parents or Guardians

Positive relationships are built on mutual trust and respect. Getting to know parents and guardians personally, yet on a professional level, helps us understand their perspectives and their approaches to particular situations. It is very important to maintain a level of professionalism that will always be focused on the needs of the student at school and at home. Here are some suggestions for doing so.

▶ Recognize that parents are a diverse grouping of individuals who will require different techniques to engage them in the educational process of their child. Some families are two-career households, some are managed by single parents, others are immigrants, and many have parents working multiple jobs.

▶ Try to understand the needs of the parent or guardian before attempting to communicate your needs as a teacher. Caregivers for students with significant disabilities may be extremely concerned about the child's safety and health while at school and not as worried about ensuring there's a change of clothes in the backpack.

▶ Be respectful of the parent or guardian and the life experiences they may have had. Not everyone has had positive school experiences themselves, so having to communicate with teachers about the disability of a child can be intimidating to some families.

▶ Send an information sheet home asking about specific likes and dislikes of the student. This will help the parent understand that you are truly interested in getting to know the child. Ask for pictures of the student in the home environment with family and friends; reciprocate with pictures of the student at school with staff and classmates.

▶ Share good things about school and the student. Try not to contact the family only when problems have occurred. Plan one day a week when you send a note or make a phone call to share something with the family.

Coordinating School and Home Expectations

One of the most sensitive and, at times, highly volatile topics of discussion can be the expectations team members—both parents and school personnel—have for students with significant disabilities. The IEP document will help guide the team in its focus on the needs of the student, but it will be necessary at times to address potentially conflicting expectations between home and school. The following are tips for avoiding unnecessary conflict in this area.

▶ Provide information to the parent regarding the district's promotion policies as students move from grade to grade. Misconceptions often occur. One parent we encountered thought that her child had to remain in kindergarten for multiple years until he had learned all the material necessary for advancement to first grade. It is the responsibility of the teacher and school administrators to explain to parents or guardians the promotion process for students with significant disabilities.

▶ Provide information regarding the grading system being used as well as progress reports on IEP goals, and ultimately provide the parent or guardian with written criteria for graduating with a diploma, certificate of completion, or certificate of attendance.

▶ As stated earlier in this book, students with significant disabilities typically do not progress through the same developmental sequences as students without disabilities. Parents may not be aware of the unique developmental style of their child. Keep parents and guardians informed of the progress students are making.

▶ Determine as a team when it is important to move on from a sequenced curriculum to a focus on functional outcomes. For example, a student with significant disabilities may not ever know the names of colors; however, learning the meaning of a few key colors in the community such as green for go and red for stop would be a functional and meaningful outcome of the student's learning. If it is apparent that the student will not likely learn the letters of the alphabet, perhaps it is possible to move on to recognition of the letters in the student's name or recognition of him- or herself in a picture. By demonstrating positive outcomes in the learning environment, teachers can help parents understand that education will not be sequential but it will be functional.

▶ It is also important for school personnel and home caregivers to discuss consistently age-appropriate social interactions for the student. Identifying peer groups in the family and community is helpful when the student requires assistance to establish relationships. Families may tend to keep students with significant disabilities with younger-aged children, thinking that they are developmentally similar. The school must take steps to ensure that the student with significant disabilities is engaging in social activities with students of the same age or interests. The following are ways to encourage age-appropriate social interactions with peers at home.
  a. Encourage the parent or guardian to identify other children in and near the family such as siblings, cousins, neighbors, and so on that may be close in age to the student. Help facilitate and identify possible friends without disabilities that families and the student could invite for a visit or a social outing.
  b. Be a resource for the family in developing communication aids or other supports to encourage peer interactions at home.
  c. Provide information to the family about neighborhood centers, after-school recreation programs, local church or community support groups, and so on. Often, a call to these agencies in advance will allow them to prepare for the participation of a student with significant disabilities.

Ongoing Communication Strategies

When asked, educators will report that one of the biggest obstacles to establishing consistent communication strategies is time. In addition, and especially in urban areas, a significant barrier to communication is language or culture. Also, consideration may need to be given to parents or guardians who are unable to read.

▶ The following strategies are offered as methods to establish quality communication that can occur naturally between home and school.

   a. Ask the parent or guardian which method of communication would work best for him or her. Offer choices including phone calls, voicemail messages, written notes on paper, e-mail messages, and so on.

   b. Use a notebook or three-ring binder to keep track of information regarding the student's daily needs and any other significant information that would be helpful to related service providers and other teachers working with the student. They can also enter information here so that everyone is aware of the student's current needs.

   c. Develop, print, and copy a template that reflects the issues requiring ongoing communication between home and school (see Figure 9.1). Keep these in student folders near the entrance to the classroom for ease of use at the end of the day.

   d. Find out if the parent or guardian transports the student to or from school. If so, use the brief moments before or after school to connect with him or her. Also, invite the parent or guardian to school for special occasions in the student's classroom or for all-school events.

   e. Consider home visits once per year.

▶ If an interpreter is needed to communicate in the parent or guardian's native language, including American Sign Language, try to find someone at school that could help with this. If there is no one on the school staff that can assist you, find out about the resources in your school district for providing interpreters. In addition, see if the student has siblings who could help direct you to an adult family member or neighbor who might be able to assist parents or guardians in communicating with the school.

▶ Parents or guardians who are unable to read will likely be reluctant to share that fact with a teacher. Look for signs that the parent is struggling with written communication. You might see this in the notes he or she may try to write, in how he or she responds to written questions, in how the student's homework is returned, in how school forms are completed, or in the fact that forms are not returned at all. Talk to the parent or guardian, and if you feel comfortable, address the issue with him or her; your school may have resources to assist in this area. If it appears that there is a reluctance to discuss the matter, change your communication strategies to verbal, either in person or on the phone. Ask the school secretary to contact the parent or guardian and complete required forms over the telephone.

▶ Pictures are worth a thousand words. Use visuals in your written communications, such as in a classroom newsletter. Pictures help those unable to read and those too busy to read a lot of text.

▶ Make use of the student's communication device. Program it so that the student can communicate information to the parent such as, "Please remember to pack my lunch for the field trip tomorrow."

IEP Team Meetings

The structure and rules of IEP team meetings can sometimes be cumbersome for parents or guardians. They might also be intimidated by the size of the

Figure 9.1 Home/School Communication Form

Student Name: _____   Date: _____

Topic	Question/Comment	Response/Date
School Activities		
Home/Community Activities		
Health Issues		
Equipment		
Supplies		
Behavior		
Other:		
Other:		

student's team, which is typically larger than average as it includes the many service providers that may be working with a student with significant disabilities. In addition, students may be making very slow progress, and that can be difficult for parents and guardians to hear every year. It is also important to note that IEP team meetings are not parent–teacher conferences; the focus here is on planning and ensuring that all members of the team understand the student's current abilities and goals for the coming year. The following strategies are intended to help you empathize with the needs of parents and guardians as you plan for the student's IEP team meeting.

▶ Carefully review the student's current IEP, paying special attention to the section that describes the concerns of the parent about the student's education. Decide if those concerns have been addressed during the year, and be prepared to discuss them with the parent or guardian at the time of scheduling the next IEP team meeting. Then, if the parent or guardian feels further discussion is necessary, it can be talked about during the meeting.

▶ Plan to start the meeting by talking about the student's strengths. Provide parents with positive things that their son or daughter can do before you discuss concerns or needs.

▶ Be aware of any issues that school staff or families may have before the meeting. Find out in advance what the parent or guardian views as the most important goals for the student. Include those things in any drafted documents that may be created prior to the meeting. If necessary, set the stage by communicating with everyone before a meeting. When the meeting is in session, listen to concerns, and recognize that the parent or guardian is knowledgeable about the needs of the student. Also, ask important questions, and be flexible. Make sure everyone has a chance to speak. It is also important to be a good listener. Everyone's ideas and concerns need to be heard. Restate what you have heard to make sure you understood correctly.

▶ Avoid the use of educational jargon. It has been said that special education has an alphabet soup vocabulary because of all the abbreviations and acronyms that are used. Use terms that can be easily understood by parents or guardians.

▶ Invite the parent or guardian to comment on another team member's contribution; the meeting should flow as a conversation, with all participants freely exchanging ideas and observations. Finally, honor the parent or guardian's time by starting the meeting as scheduled and facilitating quality discussion in a timely manner.

Parent–Teacher Conferences

The purpose of parent–teacher conferences is primarily to share information about the student's progress at school and at home; it is generally not the time to conduct an IEP team meeting. Parents and guardians want to see the learning environment for their child, to look at some of their child's work, and to talk about how the child is doing in school. Teachers want to display to best advantage the learning environment and the activities completed in the classroom and to talk about the child's progress at home. Conferences should therefore be a win–win situation. But sometimes conflicts do occur. The following suggestions are intended to assist you in achieving positive outcomes to parent–teacher conferences.

► Honor the time frame and the schedule. Cover the most important issues first, and remember that conferences are not IEP team meetings. Write down a few notes after the conference has ended; taking notes during the meeting may be intimidating to parents.

► Use a table where all participants are viewed as equal participants in the conference—round is best, or a table where no one sits at the head. Briefly review the issues to be discussed, ensuring that the parent or guardian contributes to the topics that are selected.

► Encourage parents to bring a list of questions or concerns—or even provide one to you in advance of the conference so that you can prepare. In the same way, provide the parent or guardian with a list of your questions in advance so that he or she can come prepared for discussion. Bring lots of work samples that show things the student has done.

► Consider having the student participate in the conference. Using the student's communication system, visual strategies, or assistive technology discussed in previous chapters, develop methods for the student to participate by showing the work he or she has done or by having the student ask questions such as, "How am I doing?"

10

Transition

At various times during their development, students will move from one learning environment to another. Examples of these advances are the transition from birth-to-3 services to the public school system, movement from kindergarten routines to an elementary school day, movement from elementary school to middle school expectations, and movement from school activities to postsecondary expectations such as daily living and work routines. It is necessary to anticipate and prepare for the needs of our students as they transition through these typical stages of learning.

Chapter Outline

- Parent and Student Involvement
- Transition in Early Development
- School-Age Transitions
- Identifying Adaptive Equipment Needs
- Developing Postsecondary Goals
- Planning a Coordinated Set of Activities to Help Meet Postsecondary Goals
- Determining Community Resources

Parent and Student Involvement

It is important to actively involve parents, families, and students in the educational decisions regarding transition. Connecting families with community

resources early in the student's educational career will help maintain continuity of services as the student gets older.

▶ Work with families and students to determine preferences and interests. Collaborate on increasing students' active involvement in school and community activities such as the YMCA, church groups, volunteering, and so on.

▶ Work with families and students to determine educational goals that will impact the various aspects of transition. Social skill development may not be a priority in kindergarten because of the many and varied opportunities for young children to be together. However, in later elementary and middle school years, developing appropriate social skills will be a priority for many students with significant disabilities.

▶ Encourage parents to practice self-determination skills with their child. Making choices, establishing preferences, and developing relationships are fundamental rights for all persons. When the student reaches the age of majority, parents will need to consider issues surrounding guardianship or partial guardianship for their child. Recognizing the inherent rights of the individual will help guide decision making during this transition period.

Transition in Early Development

For all children, rapid change and development typically occur in the early months and years of life. For students with significant disabilities, there will most likely be multiple transition services that have occurred prior to the start of elementary school. As teachers, we should be aware of them. Listed below are some of these transition services.

▶ Primary medical care to birth-to-3 services: Students with significant disabilities and their families have likely had experience with medical care facilities, doctors, nurses, therapists, case managers, and even social workers from the time of birth or from the time of the injury that caused the disability. Early medical care is generally followed by service from a birth-to-3 agency, where educational services are guided by IDEIA, Part B. An Individual Family Service Plan (IFSP) is developed to address delays in development, and therapy services are often provided to help the child make progress with speech and motor skills.

▶ Birth-to-3 agency to public schools: At or near the age of 3, the child is typically referred to the local public school district for an evaluation due to suspected special education needs. This transition can be difficult for parents as they begin to learn the language of special education that includes terms like disability, programs, performance levels, and so forth. This time of transition is the major shift from a medical model of care to educational services. Parents may be used to services being provided in their home or day care setting, and at this point must consider the possibility of sending their child to school.

▶ Early childhood to first grade: The biggest transition at this time is the dramatic change in routine shared by children with and without disabilities. For students with significant disabilities, however, it is important to involve the family in planning for a full day of school, 5 days a week.

School-Age Transitions

In the course of the school years, students with and without disabilities go through predictable transitions as they move through grades. As teachers, planning for the transition needs of our students should be ongoing and should include some of the aspects below.

▶ It is important to ensure that the necessary adaptive equipment is available to the student in the next grade or in the next school if moving to a middle or high school setting.

▶ Be sure to consider the involvement of the student in IEP planning activities. Students are required to be invited to their IEP team meeting at the age of 16. However, they can be involved in the process sooner, and it is important to work with the parent to determine when it is appropriate for the student to attend these meetings.

▶ Facilitate collaboration between previous teachers and yourself as well as the support staff so the needs of the student can be shared and discussed before the transition occurs. Teachers can also discuss specific teaching and behavior strategies that are successful.

▶ Provide an opportunity for students to visit a new school if they will be making a change between grade levels. See if the school provides a visitation day for students, and make sure that your students are included.

Identifying Adaptive Equipment Needs

As discussed previously, your students will likely be using various types of adapted equipment to assist them during the school day. To ensure that the equipment is available to the student as they transition between grades or to different schools, consider the following:

▶ When the type of equipment that is required for student achievement and participation is determined, it must be written into the IEP. This documentation helps to ensure that students will have access to the tools they need to be successful in the next learning environment.

▶ School staff members should consider the student's growth over time in order to anticipate the need for larger seating and standing equipment in the classroom.

▶ If the student uses an augmentative communication device, school staff members can assist with the documentation required to purchase the equipment through the student's medical insurance company.

▶ As students transition from school to adult living, the provider of adult services will be responsible for ensuring that the student has the items that are required. It is important to identify the provider of those services while the student is still in high school so that appropriate planning can occur.

Developing Postsecondary Goals

IDEIA requires that a transition plan be in place for students with disabilities at the age of 16, and some states have adopted regulations to begin transition planning at age 14. The student's transition plan must include measurable postsecondary goals in the areas of training or education, employment, and independent living skills when appropriate. Teachers at all levels should be aware of what students will need in the future and help them develop these skills.

▶ Measurable postsecondary goals are based on age-appropriate assessment. Transition assessment is an ongoing process that considers the student's strengths, areas of interest, self-determined preferences, and individual needs. Transition assessment can be formal or informal. Standardized assessment tools are available; consult with your local special education department to determine which methods are typically used in your school district.

▶ Measurable postsecondary goals reflect what the student wants to do after high school. Between ages 14 and 16, IEP goals should be developed with specific objectives that will help the student gain skills for independence after graduation. The progress toward meeting these goals should be reviewed each year by the IEP team.

▶ Postsecondary goals or outcomes are not the same as annual IEP goals. The annual IEP goals and objectives are developed *after* the measurable postsecondary goals or outcomes have been determined. The annual goals should be connected to the postsecondary goals or outcomes and help the student focus on the education, employment, and independent living outcomes that are expected.

Planning a Coordinated Set of Activities to Help Meet Postsecondary Goals

Transitioning is a lifelong process, and helping students learn needed skills should be the responsibility of every teacher—not just the secondary or transition teacher. As teachers of students with significant disabilities, we must provide repeated practice and help them build independence throughout their lives. The following are suggestions for doing so.

▶ Many functional skills are embedded throughout the curriculum and school day. Consciously include functional learning objectives in your lesson plans. For example, in kindergarten morning-circle time, during a discussion of the weather, the teacher can actively engage the student with a significant disability by having him or her choose the appropriate outerwear from two pictures.

▶ Transition skills should be developed throughout the student's school career. As mentioned earlier, elementary-age students should learn about career awareness and school jobs. In middle school, students should begin to explore careers through job shadowing and experiences. Then, in high school, students should continue to increase job experiences and awareness of requirements for specific career paths.

▶ Self-determination should be incorporated into the ongoing learning of every student. Build self-determination strategies into your lessons as students get older, and begin to set transition goals for their lives after they leave school. Train and work with students to lead their own IEP and transition meetings. See Figure 5.2 for helpful ideas to build in functional transition skills throughout the school years.

▶ Consider the courses of study that students will require as they work toward post-secondary goals. For students with significant disabilities, developing skills in the area of independent living will likely be a priority, as will building the necessary prerequisite skills to work successfully in assisted employment settings.

Determining Community Resources

As students approach graduation, the care and services they received from public schools will shift to the adult services department of the local county that is governed by the state of residence. This transition moves the student from entitlement (services that must be provided under state and federal law) to non-entitlement or eligibility criteria (student might be eligible for adult services, but the services are not guaranteed). The following suggestions will help ensure a smooth transition to adult services.

▶ Become knowledgeable about your state or county adult services division. Visit websites, and contact agencies for informational packets or pamphlets you can share with parents. See Figure 10.1 for a sample form you can use to collect data on local agencies and their services. Also, find out if your school district has a transition teacher or a vocational or job coach to assist you and your students with transition services.

▶ Be aware of, and share with families, the fact that adult agencies providing services may have waiting lists. Periodically check the length of waiting lists, and consider that there may be a possible gap in services as you conduct the transition planning activities.

▶ By law, local education agencies are required to invite the adult agencies that will be working with the student to the IEP team meeting. Consent from the parent may be required. Check your state's special education policies.

▶ Invite people from your local agencies to speak to a group of students and parents about the services provided to adults with disabilities. Also, some county agencies—at times in conjunction with schools—will provide transition fairs for families and students with disabilities. These are typically offered in the fall.

▶ In addition to routines of daily living and job skills, students also must have access to recreation and leisure activities in the community. Establishing the student's preferences and the activities that he or she enjoys will help determine the appropriate community resources.

Figure 10.1 Transition Services

Web Page Review/Phone Interview Guide

Name of Organization: _____

Web Address: _____

Local Address: _____

Phone Number: _____ Fax Number: _____

Name of Contact Person: _____ Date Contacted: _____

Information:

Type of Clients Served: _____

_____

_____

Services Offered:

_____   _____

_____   _____

_____   _____

Eligibility Requirements: _____

_____

_____

Application Process: _____

_____

_____

Fees/Special Rates for Services: _____

_____

Transportation (if available): _____

_____

■ References

Anderson, V. A., Catroppa, C., Morse, S., Haritou, F., & Rosenfeld, J. V. (2005, December). Functional plasticity or vulnerability after early brain injury? *Pediatrics, 116*(6), 1374–1382.

Ayers, W. (2001). *To teach: The journey of a teacher.* New York: Teachers College Press.

Brown, L., Branston, M. B., Hamre-Nietupski, S., Pumpian, I., Certo, N., & Gruenewald, L. (1979). A strategy for developing chronological-age-appropriate and functional curricular content for severely handicapped adolescents and young adults. *Journal of Special Education, 13*(1), 81–90.

Brown, L., Shiraga, B., York, J., Zanella, K., & Rogan, P. (1984). *The discrepancy analysis technique in programs for students with severe handicaps.* Madison: University of Wisconsin & Madison Metropolitan School District. The production of this version was supported by grants for the WI Dept of Public Instruction and the USDOE, OSERS, OSEP, Program for Children with Severe Disabilities to the Wisconsin School Inclusion Project.

Falvey, M., Forest, M., Pearpoint, J., & Rosenberg, R. (1997). *All my life's a circle. Using the tools: Circles, MAPS, and PATHS.* Toronto, Ont., Canada: Inclusion Press.

Ferguson, D., & Baumgart, D. (1991). Partial participation revisited. *Journal of the Association for Persons with Severe Handicaps (JASH), 16*(4), 218–227.

Ford, A., Davern, L., & Schnorr, R. (2001). Learners with significant disabilities: Curricular relevance in an era of standards-based reform. *Remedial and Special Education, 22,* 214–221.

Giangreco, M., Cloninger, C. J., & Iverson, V. S. (2005). *Choosing options and accommodations for children: A guide to educational planning for students with disabilities* (2nd ed.). Baltimore: Paul H. Brookes.

Giangreco, M., Edelman, S., Luiselli, T., & MacFarland, S. (1997). Helping or hovering? *Exceptional Children, 64,* 7–18.

Kagan, S. (1989/1990, December/January). The structural approach to cooperative learning [electronic version]. *Educational Leadership, 47*(4), 12–15.

Kluth, P. (2003). *You're going to love this kid: Teaching student with autism in the inclusive classroom.* Baltimore: Paul H. Brookes.

Kluth, P., Straut, D., & Biklen, D. (Eds). (2003). *Access to academics for all students: Critical approaches to inclusive curriculum, instruction, and policy.* Mahwah, NJ: Erlbaum.

Menchetti, B. M., & Sweeney, M. A. (1995). *Person-centered planning: Technical assistance packet* (No. 5). Gainesville: University of Florida.

National Center for Educational Statistics. (2006, January). *Digest of Educational Statistics,* Table 51 (Fall 1989–Fall 2004). Retrieved June 18, 2008, from http://nces.ed.gov/programs/digest/d05/tables/dt05_051.asp.

O'Brien, J. (1987). A guide to lifestyle planning. In T. Bellamy & B. Wilcox (Eds.), *The activity catalogue: A programming guide for youth and adults with severe disabilities* (pp. 75–88). Baltimore: Paul H. Brookes.

Orelove, F., Sobsey, D., & Silberman, K. (2004). *Educating children with multiple disabilities: A collaborative approach* (4th ed.). Baltimore: Paul H. Brookes.

Pitonyak, D. (n.d.). *7—Questions to guide the development of a support plan: Difficult behaviors result from unmet needs.* Retrieved September 1, 2007, from http://dimagine.com/page63.html.

Reed, P. & Lahm, E. (2005). *A resource guide for teachers and administrators about assistive technology.* Madison: Wisconsin Assistive Technology Initiative. Available online at http://www.wati.org/products/freematerials.html.

Ryndak, D., & Alper, S. (2003). *Curriculum and instruction for students with moderate and severe disabilities in inclusive settings* (2nd ed.). Needham Heights, MA: Allyn & Bacon.

Shevin, M. (1987). *The language of us and them* (poem). Unpublished manuscript. Available online at http://www.shevin.org/articles-usthem.html.

Tomlinson, C. (1995). *How to differentiate instruction in a mixed-ability classroom.* Alexandria, VA: Association for Supervision and Curriculum Development.

Udvari-Solner, A. (1996). Examining teacher thinking: Constructing a process to design curricular adaptations. *Remedial and Special Education, 17,* 245–254.

WATI Assessment Forms. (2004). Wisconsin Assistive Technology Initiative.

Wehman, P. (2006). *Life beyond the classroom: Transition strategies for young people with disabilities.* Baltimore: Paul H. Brookes.

Wehman, P., & Kragel, J. (2003). *Functional curriculum: For elementary, middle, and secondary age students with special needs* (2nd ed.). Austin, TX: Pro-Ed.

Wisconsin School Inclusion Project: Team Planning Packet (1995). *Climate and peer supports: Classroom climate checklist.* Portage, WI: CESA 5 (Cooperative Educational Service Agency).

Zabala, J. (2005). *Using the SETT framework to level the learning field for students with disabilities.* Retrieved June 20, 2008, from http://www.ode.state.or.us/initiatives/elearning/nasdse/settintrogeneric2005.pdf.

Suggested Website Resources

Community Resources for Independence. Independent Living: www.crinet.org/dignity.php

Provincial Integration Support Program: www.pisp.ca

Wisconsin Assistive Technology Initiative: www.wati.org

■ Index

CORWIN PRESS